Electronic Evidence Management

FROM CREATION THROUGH LITIGATION

By Mary Mack, Esq. and Steve Pattison

Published by Discovery Center of Excellence

ISBN 0-9725542-5-4

Printed in the United States of America

PREFACE

We are pleased to present you with Electronic Evidence Management, the latest in our series of guides for discovery, litigation readiness and evidence management strategies in an era of electronic data.

This guide is the first to examine a complete lifecycle of evidence management — from the moment any document is created, to its transition to record or potential evidence, through to the electronic discovery process. Advances in document management within enterprises, combined with the legal expertise and technology of electronic discovery professionals, now make it possible to unify both document management and electronic evidence management under a single business process.

The benefits can be profound. When there is a complete lifecycle for managing evidence, directed by a well thought-out business process, corporations are spared the unnecessary burden of preserving every single record 'just in case'. At the same time, they have a clear and defensible policy and process for identifying and preserving potentially responsive data — culling it from the vast herd of electronic information.

Proactively identifying and preserving potential evidence, in turn, reduces time and energy spent in reactive, fire drill-style responses to each and every matter, regulatory audit or other event calling for information records. Moreover, correct management of responsive records reduces the risk of spoliation and subsequent sanctions, many of which can be severe.

This guide also includes updated information from the book *A Process of Illumination: The Practical Guide to Electronic Discovery,* including sample forms and concrete examples that apply to both respondents and requesters of electronic evidence. We also show how thinking proactively in a digital age — rather than reacting to each individual litigation — can streamline, simplify and reduce costs involved in electronic discovery. With these updates, we believe we have created an informative yet highly practical guide for managing data and electronic discovery as part of a complete evidence management solution.

No book on the subject of evidence management and electronic discovery can be complete without acknowledging the contribution of the pioneers in the field: Dennis Kennedy, Bonnie Poindexter, Jonathan Redgrave, Joan Feldman, Michael Anderson, Michael Bawden, Richard Lazar, Larry Johnson, Tom Howe, Ken Withers, Florinda Baldridge, John Jesson, Tim Stevens, Laura Kibbe, Kevin Esposito, Jim Daley, Denise Howell, Michael Clark, George Socha, Michael Overly, Mike Arkfield, Michael Rhoden, Jason Ray, Chuck Kellner, Southern District Judge Shira Scheindlin, Matt Yarbrough, Tom Stevens, Brian Ingram, Alan Gahtan, Michael Daniec, Bill Adams, Prashant Dubey and Tom O'Conner.

We also want to acknowledge and thank our team of contributing authors: Matt Deniston, Julia Wotipka, Therese Adlhoch Smith, and Charlene Brownlee. For writing and editorial contributions, the FIOS team acknowledges Renate Lewin, Kate Kockler, Jeri Owen, Keith Lipman and Integrity Design.

You may have specific questions not covered within the scope of this guide. Because electronic discovery and evidence management are undergoing rapid growth and change, new concepts and issues are constantly emerging. We always welcome your inquiries and are particularly interested in your stories, successful or otherwise. Contact us in the manner most convenient for you:

Email us at guide@fiosinc.com.
Call us toll-free at (877) 700-3467 or direct at (503) 265-0700
Fax us at (503) 265-0001.

You can also visit web portals and resources that we participate in, including **www.discoveryresources.org**

Or write to us: Fios, Inc.

> Attn: **Electronic Evidence Management**
> 921 SW Washington Street, Suite 850
> Portland, OR 97205

Look for updates at **www.fiosinc.com**

TABLE OF CONTENTS

1

THE EVIDENCE MANAGEMENT
LIFECYCLE

Two powerful trends in information management are converging: electronic records retention for business purposes, including regulatory compliance, and electronic records preservation and discovery for legal matters.

Traditionally managed as separate aspects of corporate governance — records management for business purposes and evidence management for legal matters — both can be much more efficient when linked. They can be unified under a shared process-oriented approach, leveraging records management best practices and document capture technologies, while satisfying the preservation and discovery requirements of legal matters.

The synergy couldn't be more natural — and valuable to the business. On one side of the equation, corporations already know they need to capture and retain records. On the other side, Corporate Legal Departments (CLDs) know lawsuits are virtually inevitable in today's litigious environment.

Together, records management and electronic discovery enable an unprecedented way to make evidence management a proactive, rather than a reactive, exercise: the Evidence Management Lifecycle![1]

---

[1] For timely discussion of the importance of records policies and electronic discovery for today's corporations, see "The Price of Flawed Electronic Discovery," Forrester Research, Inc., May 20, 2005.

SCENARIO:

It's time for the executive administrative assistant to clear the clutter in the top floor office. He gathers up print-outs of reams of everyday correspondence, contracts, memos, completed litigation, court rulings, patent filings, complaints about the product, HR disputes and more. He notifies management of his intent to archive and eventually destroy, to receive authorization that this is the right thing to do.

He takes everything down to the file room, where kindly Ms. Records smiles and nods, and reassuringly takes charge of the physical body of evidence. (Because that's what it may eventually become — evidence.) All is well.

Then a matter arises. Litigation is looming. A legal hold is placed on all potentially responsive records. Of course, the old boxed records are immediately requested from the offsite repository. Unfortunately, some have already been destroyed according to the company's proscribed cycle of retention and destruction, because it was not communicated to the outside storage vendor that a legal hold was in effect. Or have they all been destroyed in every format? Some of the relevant documents are still showing up on the company's servers. Some reside on current users' desktop, albeit as "hidden" data. Other files, used as evidence in a related case three years ago, may be sitting with outside counsel — but we're not sure. Too bad, because it would have saved time and money to re-use the work product.

During a deposition, opposing counsel has also found out there may be relevant voice mails and instant messages responsive to the matter. Unfortunately, unaware of the impending proceedings, IT has destroyed the digital records (or failed to capture them in the first place). IT received a memo about the importance of preserving potential evidence, but they were in the middle of a server upgrade, new software had recently crashed, a new CIO was reorganizing the departments.... and so forth.

> *Meanwhile, IT has redeployed the computers used by the disgruntled plaintiffs — without capturing a mirror image of their hard drives. The opposing counsel is asking for discovery and production. The judge has set a timeline for discovery and production. But you don't even know what you have or where it is. Not amused at your requests for extensions or protestations that this is all you can produce, the judge grants sanctions in favor of the plaintiff.*
>
> *Boxes from the repository? That's just the tip of the iceberg in an era of electronic discovery.*

LESSON LEARNED:

> We may not like it or understand it all, but in today's world, potentially responsive material resides everywhere. The probability of its use for adversarial litigation — or even to support positive matters such as mergers, acquisitions and earning certifications-requires a cohesive records retention and document management policy that includes hard copy, electronic documents, digital communications and everything in-between.

"The wake-up call has been issued: Companies must proactively prepare for electronic discovery and create policies and procedures around email usage and archiving or pay the price."
—Barry Murphy, *The Price Of Flawed Electronic Discovery,* Forrester Research, Inc., *May 2005*

Even without their use for legal issues, corporate records represent valuable information, the intellectual capital of the business. Document management and records retention should not be primarily a failsafe for litigation — it is simply good business practice.

War stories like the one above hold of the lessons of what to do and what not to do when litigation impacts an enterprise.

We have peppered this guide with similar anecdotes and examples in an effort to keep it grounded in practicality. Names and functions have been changed to protect the identities of the subjects of these stories except where participants ended up in a cited law opinion.

Of course, in addition to technology and right practices, it is the people involved in compliance and electronic discovery who will make or break success. You need people who can communicate from inside counsel, outside counsel, litigation support, client IT, business units, records management, compliance and finance domains. Interpersonal communication skills aside, these groups have significantly different vocabularies and objectives. Make sure your team has someone who can facilitate trust among the various stakeholders to move your project forward.

> **"It is the combination of sound policies and procedures, education of employees and stakeholders, and supporting software that will allow companies to manage the risks associated with litigation."**
> —Barry Murphy, *The Price Of Flawed Electronic Discovery,* Forrester Research, Inc., *May 2005*

Are We There Yet?

The premise of this book is that electronic evidence is quickly becoming the norm, and it is something that legal professionals and their clients cannot ignore. On the other hand, let's not forget that plenty of hardcopy records still exist and continue to be created. Technology adoption in the evidence management arena has progressed steadily over the past 30 years and can be summarized into three primary phases:

1) **Storage of "Finished Good" paper documents,** first localized in file rooms, then shipped to document storage facilities

2) **Selective retention of Finished Good documents** in electronic repositories (via scanning or other digital capture)

3) **Content capture via departmental content applications** (matter-centric collaboration, contract management, case management, etc.) where content is captured electronically as *it is being created*

Most companies are somewhere along the midpoint of this technology adoption curve. Changes in regulatory exposure and technology advances are causing rapid, industry-wide movements to accelerate investment in evidence and document management technologies. An evolutionary process from paper retention, to electronic data, to comprehensive records management, and finally to adoption of a complete Evidence Management Lifecycle process, is what will distinguish corporate leaders going forward.

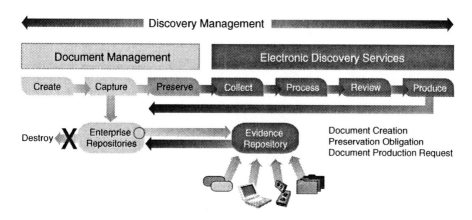

The maturation of records management as a disciplined IT practice essential to business operations enables a complete evidence management lifecycle that is proactive. Corporations can streamline and speed their ability to respond to litigation. They can link the enterprise capability for records capture with evidence preservation, processing and production in electronic discovery.

Evolution of Business Records Management

At one time, capturing and storing business documents was relatively straightforward. Everything was originally in hard copy, whether as formal documents or scribbled notes. Those documents that were deemed to be worth keeping were stored and remained available. Businesses would keep these documents for a specified period of time (or merely until the file cabinets were bulging), then box them up and send them to a storage facility.

In the most structured firms, boxes were numbered and indexed to indicate what they contained, before being shipped to a storage facility. In smaller or more casual businesses, boxes may simply have been stored blind (i.e., no destruction index) at a local warehouse. This was not an "enterprise" undertaking as we understand the term today, but at least it was a methodology that worked most of the time.

If litigation arose, any extant boxes could be retrieved and physically searched for responsive material. The point here is that relevant content was easy to determine. In the reality of those days, you simply asked the actors involved and they pointed you to the relevant filling cabinet or box that is offsite.

Tedious and time consuming, perhaps. Not to mention the paper cuts. But it was nothing compared to what we have now, in an electronic age. Any document (these days, "document" almost always means an electronic record) may eventually become evidence. But do you have to save everything? And if so, where?

The Impact of Email

In the paper world, all content could become evidence. Therefore it was usually categorized or indexed, as discussed above. The problem in the desktop PC era is that content is no longer being categorized or indexed. Instead it sits on people inboxes or network file shares. As a result the amount of effort to find relevant content has increased remarkably. Additionally, people now put into email comments that they would never have put in a paper memo — the filters of the paper systems are gone. This free-wheeling activity opens people up to lots of liability. In the paper world, there was a filter for what to keep. Basically you were forced to deal with your paper because it occupied space. With electronic content, people just let it build up because it does not affect them — or so they think.

What is a Record and How Long do I Have to Keep It?

At its simplest, a record is evidence of a business transaction or communication. According to the ISO 15489 definition: "A record is information created, received, and maintained as evidence by an organization or person in the transaction of business, or in the pursuance of legal obligations, regardless of media."[2]

As we'll show later in this guide, records that are electronic can exist in many different formats and locations, and like rabbits, keep replicating. A record could also be a conventional document in hard copy. In today's digital age, hard copy may be scanned and captured electronically as well.

Records management is a systematic discipline for managing the retention and destruction of all relevant content and data assets related to a specific business issue/project. Over the years, records management has evolved from a clerical task to a vital business operation embodying best practices, policy development and employee training. The latest enterprise information management technologies have made it vastly easier to capture, organize and store records, and to establish a stringent document management policy.

---

[2] "The Challenge Of Electronic Records Corporate Compliance – From E-Mail To I-Pods," by Charlene Brownlee And Melissa Cozart. Quoted in **Law Journal Newsletters — The Corporate Counselor**, June 2005 Issue. ©2005 Alm Properties, Inc.

Increased stringency in records management is in part driven by recent corporate scandals and concerns about corporate governance. For example, the Sarbanes-Oxley Act imposes various retention requirements on publicly traded companies and imposes liability on their chief executive and financial officers for violation of such requirements.

How long certain records must be retained is also controlled. Audit firms must maintain all work papers related to an audit or review for a period of five years, with fines and/or imprisonment for violations. Accountants of securities issuers must retain records relevant to audits or reviews for a period of seven years.

Records management best practices will dictate how long other kinds of documents are kept. For example, it might be standard to purge emails after 90 days, or shred tax records after 7 years and so forth.

However, the overriding principle is that when litigation is likely, any routine destruction policy must be suspended for potentially responsive records.

For more on records, records management and legal implications of records management, excellent materials and comprehensive information is available from **www.fulbright.com.**

But I'm Not a Records Management Expert!

Companies aren't in the business of being records managers or electronic discovery experts. They want to (and should) focus on their core business. And, they should not be managing records simply for fear of litigation, but doing it for necessary business objectives. It's just that if you have your records in order, improved litigation readiness naturally follows.

Just as with any other important business function, records management can be achieved with help from third party professionals. For example, ARMA International, a non-profit association for information manage-ment professionals **(www.arma.org)** is a rich source of information and help, including lists of vendors providing records management assistance. Records and information management specialist firms are available to help collect the statutory policies and emerging retention rulings that apply to a business and define an appropriate records and retention policy.

Of course, any records program must have a companion policy for legal holds to enforce preservation duty if litigation seems likely. Automation and process is a benefit, but you don't want a records policy that's on auto-pilot.

What determines whether or not a particular document or email is a record is the content of the message. An email itself is not a record, but a means of delivering the message. According to Records Management expert Charlene Brownlee, every employee is now a records manager because of the proliferation of electronic communications.[3] As a result of this fact, you can never rely entirely on technology to determine whether an email is a record. Employees must be trained on what constitutes a record and how that record must be saved in accordance with the organization's records retention schedule.

For the records system to be effective, you must capture all of the content that is relevant to a given project. Without this context-based records concept, you are back to mining content from emails, file systems, and other content stores when litigation occurs. The challenge with records systems is that end users must actually participate in the system to store and identify records. Most records systems have failed in this regard. To be effective, the records system must be:

1. Easy to use — work similar today to how end users work with their file shares, c drives, etc.
2. Work as part of the email client so that users do not have to exit one environment and enter another to identify records
3. Provide offline access for laptop users, particularly in industries where key content workers are mobile

> **"Records management solutions can help support the enforcement of policies and procedures by easing the process of designating documents for archival...And services like those offered by electronic discovery service providers assist in parsing through all archived documents and analyzing them for relevancy to the case under litigation."**
> —Barry Murphy, *The Price Of Flawed Electronic Discovery,* Forrester Research, Inc., *May 2005*

---

[3] "The Challenge of Electronic Records: Corporate Compliance — From E-Mail To I-Pods," by Charlene Brownlee and Melissa Cozart. June 2005 edition of the LAW JOURNAL NEWSLETTERS – THE CORPORATE COUNSELOR. ALM Properties, Inc.

You Don't have to Preserve Everything

The whole issue of e-discovery can be scary. Sure, there is more potential evidence to find and derivative sources and volumes of data to consider than ever in the days of plain old paper documents. On the bright side, the basic rules of the court prevail. According to Laura Kibbe, Esq.:[4]

"In an attempt to appear informed and on top of our electronic discovery game, and in the era of "Zubulake," we may have overindulged complexity. E-discovery conferences abound, service providers purport to provide the hottest new "tools" for discovery, and lawyers take newly learned jargon into the courtroom. All this misses a very basic tenant of discovery: FRCP 26(a) "Required Disclosures." Neither technology nor the proposed amendments can change this basic obligation. Kibbe also notes that while e-discovery is different from traditional discovery, many of the questions remain the same as always.

"To ensure we fulfill our preservation obligations, we need to answer some basic questions.
1. What will be the court's (and my opposition's) expectation of what I need to preserve?
2. Do I believe that expectation is fair and defensible?
3. Do I believe my adjustment of their expectation is defensible?
4. Can I ensure that the actions I take to identify potentially responsive evidence will demonstrate good faith?
5. Can I ensure the processes I use to preserve evidence will maintain the evidence in an un-altered state?
6. Can I ensure that I know exactly where the evidence has been and who has accessed or interacted with it?
7. Can I demonstrate I have taken proactive steps to cease the (normal course of business) destruction of documents in order for them to be preserved?
8. Do I believe that the (imminent) discovery request will be overly burdensome for me to respond to?"

Remember that the possibility of litigation and e-discovery does NOT mean a business has to preserve every email, every document, every record forever. Instead, there should be a records management policy in place with standard capture and destruction policies to support business needs, such as compliance audits and everyday operations. The destruction

---

[4] From "WYSIWYG…Your Honor," by Laura Kibbe, Esq. Corporate Counsel Magazine, June 2005

policies need *only* be suspended for potentially responsive documents when litigation is likely. The record/document system may not need to be enterprise wide in order to be effective. Additionally, and enterprise-wide taxonomy may be overkill to address future discovery requirements. The most critical success factor for a records management system is to ensure that the technology is deployed to groups and departments that have the highest risk of litigation.

Commenting on the recent reversal of the Arthur Anderson decision and the importance of records management, the firm of Fulbright and Jaworski stated:

> "As always, the safest way to avoid civil and criminal liability is to follow records management best practices. No corporation that has acted diligently, competently and in good faith has been subject to liability. The market may evolve to the point, as it did in the pharmaceutical industry, that to demonstrate good faith an organization must make appropriate, proactive infrastructure investments to store, retain, and retrieve subject material.
>
> An effective records management program should be designed to achieve the following objectives: (1) ensure that all needed business records are retained; (2) ensure that all records that are required to be retained by statute, regulation, or contract are retained for the appropriate period of time; (3) establish litigation hold procedures to ensure that potentially responsive documents are not destroyed once litigation and/or government investigation is reasonably anticipated; and (4) establish procedures to ensure the destruction of appropriate documents as their respective retention periods expire."[5]

In other words, save what you need to manage the business, but also have a process in place that allows for preservation of files when needed for an anticipated litigation or investigation. The principal advantage of the records/document system is that when litigation happens, counsel can be quickly directed to where the relevant content can be found. As a result, the discovery process is expedited as the search and categorization

---

[5] Excerpted from Legal Update, May 31, 2005, Fulbright and Jaworski L.L.C. Find the full article, with case references, at *www.discoveryresources.com*

requirements and reduced for the e-discovery vendor, outside council, and corporate discovery team.

This brings us to the idea of building a preservation repository to capture and retain a snapshot of potentially relevant documents for later analysis, should a document production request be forthcoming. And that in turn gets us to a happy convergence made possible only by the state of technology today: Linking enterprise records management with preservation and discovery in a unified business process.

When a company already has a document management and records retention system in place, responsive information can be easily preserved, segregated and stored as needed for legal purposes. Instead of being scattered across limited point solutions, such as email archiving, voice mail capture and backup data tapes, all records (both electronic and traditional) can be uniformly handled and organized. A legally defensible process will verify that content and dates are maintained as the files move from place to place.

The benefits of an end-to-end Evidence Management Lifecycle process are manifold:

- It's easier to enforce preservation holds on responsive documents, without burdening the business, because everything is already captured. Automated technologies need only to search the repository to identify what files you need to preserve for specific needs, such as compliance audits, government investigations, litigation and so forth.

- Documents identified and produced for one matter can be stored in case of future discovery requests. You don't have to re-do the entire discovery process over again for subsequent matters.

- Instead of two siloed processes — one for business records and another for gathering evidence — both use the same underlying repository technologies in a unified process. The document management system captures and stores the document, but can easily hand off a document to the discovery lifecycle of preserve-collect-process-review-produce. Time, costs, and IT burden are reduced.

- Team collaboration is enhanced. With a single point of access instead of disparate standalone solutions, key stakeholders throughout the organization gain visibility into the current status of all legal matters.

- Security is easier to ensure when you have a consolidated repository for everything.

- Discovery end products are returned to the corporate document management/records management repository, ensuring that future discovery processes are incremental additions, not complete redo's.

Bottom line: When documents are managed in an end-to-end evidence lifecycle, from creation to litigation, you spend less time hunting for evidence. You save time and eliminate paying multiple times for the same legal process. Current work product is leveraged so you also spend less on outside counsel fees in the future. Discovery becomes a managed, sane process instead of a fire drill for each matter. You will get better and better at managing your evidence and will achieve more positive outcomes, with less pain.

2

ENSURING THE PRESERVATION OF DATA WHEN LITIGATION IS LOOMING

Regardless of where your company is on the technology adoption curve, there is still an obligation to preserve. The risks of not having a legally defensible process for preservation in place are high:

- Sanctions by courts or regulatory bodies

- Unpredictable costs (unpredictability in terms of cost, time, and risk)

- Poor outcomes in litigation

- Lack of repeatability — every matter becomes a new fire drill

The origin of the duty to preserve potential evidence arises from the common law, with courts establishing local rules for digital evidence — "Duty to Investigate and Disclose. Prior to a Fed. R. Civ. P. 26(f) conference, counsel shall review with the client the client's information management systems, including computer-based and other digital systems, in order to understand how information is stored and how it can be retrieved. To determine what must be disclosed pursuant to Fed. R. Civ. P. 26(a)(1), counsel shall further review with the client the client's information files, including currently maintained computer files as well as historical, archival, backup, and legacy computer files . . ." District of New Jersey, Local Rule 26.1(d)(1)[6]

---

[6] See the Fios webcast for more information. "Creating a Defensible and Credible Evidence Preservation/Collection Plan in the Face of Impending Litigation," *http://www.fiosinc.com/events/webcast_archive.html*

Both types of proactive demands/requirements are becoming more common. But duty to preserve exists even in the absence of a preservation letter or order. Unfortunately, the "trigger" of that duty is often unclear, and it may apply at any of several stages. Certainly, a company that endures regular litigation, such as big pharma and financial services, should know not to destroy certain kinds of information that are highly likely to become evidence.

So how do you decide what to do without over-preserving? Remember if you over-preserve you will be adding more processing, reviewing and production time, with everything scaling as it goes downstream as well.

A balancing test considers the following three factors when deciding a motion to preserve documents:

1. The level of concern the court has for the continuing existence and maintenance of the integrity of the evidence in question in the absence of an order directing preservation of the evidence

2. Any irreparable harm likely to result to the party seeking the preservation of evidence absent an order directing preservation

3. The capability of an individual, entity, or party to maintain the evidence sought to be preserved, not only as to the evidence's original form, condition or contents, but also the physical, spatial and financial burdens created by ordering evidence preservation.[7]

Although negligent e-discovery conduct has been sanctioned in all 12 federal judicial circuits[8] a survey by Judge Sheindlin indicates that the sanctions aren't arbitrary nor imposed for honest mistakes — the courts have been pretty much right on target:

"The results of our survey reveal that the profile of a typical sanctioned party is a defendant that destroys electronic information in violation of a court order, in a manner that is willful or in bad faith, or causes prejudice to the opposing party.[9]

---

[7] Capricorn Power Company, Inc. v. Siemens Westinghouse Power Corporation, Civil Action No. 01-39J, 2004 WL 870659 (W.D. Pa. April 21, 2004)

[8] "The E-discovery Missteps that Judges Love to Hate," by Paul Neale, Law Practice Today, February 2005

[9] Shira A. Scheindlin and Kanchana Wangkeo, Electronic Discovery Sanctions in the Twenty-First Century, 11 Mich. Telecomm. Tech. L. Rev. 71 (2004) available at http://www.mttlr.org/voleleven/scheindlin.pdf

Fortunately, while the duty to preserve evidence is a broad mandate, it does not require a litigant to keep every scrap of paper or electronic document. Moreover, information searches can be easily automated.

"[If it is not feasible to speak with every key player] counsel must be more creative. It may be possible to run a system-wide keyword search; counsel could then preserve a copy of each 'hit.' Although this sounds burdensome, it need not be."[10]

You can then use document management technology to preserve potentially relevant information in an evidence repository. This segregation allows document destruction systems to continue to operate, thus minimizing impact on company operations.

A caveat about preservation orders: Do not rely solely on the cooperation of employees. One of the primary reasons that electronic data is lost is ineffective communication with employees and information technology personnel.

Automating the search for information can minimize the impact of employee noncompliance with the litigation hold, but Counsel must still issue a "litigation hold" at the outset of litigation or whenever litigation is reasonably anticipated. The hold should be periodically re-issued so that new employees are aware of it, and so that it is fresh in the mind of all employees. Counsel should communicate directly with the "key players" in the litigation. As with the litigation hold, the key players should be periodically reminded that the preservation duty is still in place.

And once again, all of this becomes easier, more efficient and legally defensible when you have a complete Evidence Management Lifecycle in place. Together, document management and evidence management enable corporations to:

• Empower collaboration and discovery management through the capture of electronic documents in secure, scalable repositories.

• Meet preservation obligations when litigation is anticipated by quickly and accurately identifying relevant documents from throughout the enterprise and ensuring they are not inadvertently destroyed.

---

[10]Zubulake v. UBS Warburg, LLC, 2004 WL 1620866 (S.D.N.Y. July 20, 2004)

- Collect, process, review and deliver responsive documents through a process-oriented approach that is fast, efficient, predictable and legally defensible.

To make the preservation search defensible, Counsel must now understand what areas of the enterprise are being searched or inventoried, and with what methodology. In Morgan Stanley v. Coleman,[11] the judge was concerned about:

- Waves of backup tapes that were not disclosed in a timely manner

- Servers where email archiving was being staged prior to full deployment

- Attachments not being searched due to script error

- Hits missed by the search engine due to "hyper" case sensitivity

---

[11] Coleman (Parent) Holdings, Inc. v. Morgan Stanley & Co., Inc., 2005 WL 67071 (Fla. Cir. Ct. Mar. 1, 2005)

3

WHAT HAPPENS DURING ELECTRONIC DISCOVERY?

SCENARIO: **A high-level termination**

> *You are thinking of firing a key employee. She's been hinting that if you do, she might file an EEOC complaint. Attempting to plan ahead for a lawsuit, you email your inside and outside counsel detailing the situation, placing "attorney-client privilege" in the subject line. "My communication should now be protected," or so you think. You do fire the key employee with all of the i's dotted and t's crossed. Six months later, she files her complaint. Her counsel sends over a document request for the emails of the last year. Your attorneys put an immediate legal hold on emails and backup tapes, but the emails from six months ago have been overwritten as part of your normal document retention policy. Your IT department starts saving tapes. You are shocked to hear at trial that from the moment you sent your "privileged" email to your attorneys, you had an obligation to retain material potentially relevant to the matter.[12] Your case has taken a negative turn due to this misunderstanding of what is required and when it is required.*

---

[12] Zubulake vs. UBS Warburg LLC, No. 02 Civ. 1243, 2003 WL 21087884 (S.D.N.Y. May 13, 2003)

LESSON LEARNED:

> If you are communicating, particularly in writing and especially in email, with your attorneys about a situation which may evolve into legal proceedings, your attorneys need to start involving IT for preservation activities immediately. It is not enough to wait until you receive a formal notice.

This is where the linked systems of document management, evidence management and discovery domain expertise kick into gear. Evidence must be collected, using legally defensible methodologies, and moved into an evidence repository for processing. With a unified process and common source repository in place, this is more easily achieved.

Why Zubulake is So Important

The case of Zubulake v UBS Warburg is considered to be the first definitive case in the United States that has flushed out a wide range of electronic discovery and spoliation issues. United States District Court Judge Shira A. Scheindlin has issued five ground-breaking opinions in this case, helping to establish a baseline for electronic discovery issues in modern litigation. These issues include:

- The scope of a party's duty to preserve electronic evidence during the course of litigation;
- A counsel's duty to monitor their clients' compliance with electronic data preservation and production;
- Data sampling recommendations and guidelines.
- The ability for the disclosing party to shift the costs of restoring "inaccessible" back up tapes to the requesting party;
- The imposition of sanctions for the spoliation (or destruction) of electronic evidence.

Interestingly, while spoliation judgments were relatively rare in the era of paper discovery, they are common for electronic data. Because spoliation can be equated to perjury, the sanctions can be severe. Besides legal costs and fines, the ultimate penalty — the summary judgment-lurks for corporations that have not shown good faith in their document management and legal hold policies, or that appear to 'drag their feet' when an electronic discovery request is made. According to Records Management Policy expert Laura Kibbe of Pfizer, "Don't play 'hide the ball' with the opposition when it comes to e-evidence. Negotiate scope and need early on."

Defining Electronic Discovery

Electronic discovery is the collection, processing, review and distribution of electronic documents associated with legal and government proceedings.

"Documents," as defined in most requests for production, include email messages and associated file attachments (the email "chain"), memos, reports, plain text files, spreadsheets, digital art and photos, presentations and any other data that is created or stored on a computer, computer network or other electronic storage media.

That's the dry description.

In reality, electronic discovery also means a paradigm shift from the single dimension of traditional document discovery, into the new age of digital information. Unlike paper evidence, electronic evidence is multi-dimensional, potentially 'virtual' (i.e., not tied to or under control of a single user), and rarely can be destroyed altogether without leaving tell-tale signs that may themselves be responsive in a matter.

For example, electronic discovery includes files residing on laptops, office PCs, network servers, enterprise content and records management systems, floppy disks, Personal Digital Assistants (PDAs), CD-ROMs, DVD-ROMs, MP3 players, Blackberries, smart cell phones, backup tapes, flash memory cards and devices, other archive media, and 3rd party storage systems. Moreover, with unified messaging (i.e., Voice over IP instead of traditional telephone), voice mails become digital evidence, as collectable as email. All of this digital content generates metadata as it is forwarded, downloaded, archived, copied or moved, which can also become part of litigation.

It is this broad potential scope of the electronic discovery universe that can intimidate those new to the concept. Unlike paper evidence, electronic evidence is far more voluminous, easily replicated and distributed than hard copy, and it includes unseen metadata, chains and threads that can be more significant than the original content itself.

Electronic evidence and failure to manage it properly is the source of much unnecessary cost and risk. "More money is probably spent litigating electronic discovery problems than in litigating class actions," said Ken Withers, senior education attorney at the Washington-based Federal Judicial Center, the research arm of the U.S. courts. "This is part of potentially every case in the 21st Century."

Because of the differences between traditional discovery and electronic discovery, spoliation is a bigger issue than it ever was with conventional documents. Without a clear records retention policy and defensible evidence preservation and collection policy, spoliation risks abound. Pleading ignorance will not win you any points with the judge, as was demonstrated in Perelman vs. Morgan Stanley.

Organizational Litigation Readiness

Assess your litigation readiness. Ask yourself some questions about whether you have preservation protocols in place, collection methodology, review and production capabilities. Imagine that you have a "business ending" lawsuit and need to collect, review and produce within 30 days. Who would be on your team? Who understands the electronic data systems? Who controls people's time in IT? What segments of the business have record retention systems? Which of the outside counsel is experienced in preservation, review and production?

What's Important for Individuals to Consider?

The hazards and opportunities of digital evidence vary depending on your role or position within an organization and which side of the litigation you're on. Here are some examples of how the new realities of electronic discovery can impact you.

Executive Management

SCENARIO: **Shredding electronic data**

> *The Attorney General has been engaging you in conversations about practices at your firm. No papers have been received by your firm yet. Your executive team is getting nervous. News reporters are calling to run down rumors in the business press. You've heard hallway discussions about "Evidence Eliminator," a "wiping" program that is the electronic equivalent of the paper shredder. It is supposed to really delete files, not the kind of deletions the hapless Arthur Andersen people accomplished.[13] Should you intervene to stop employees from wiping their drives, or would it be better to look the other way?*

---

[13] Although the Arthur Andersen decision was ultimately reversed, it was done so on the grounds of improper and overly broad instructions to the jury, not on the issue of electronic evidence retention policies and spoliation. In the meantime, the whole debacle of Enron and Arthur Andersen's inconsistently applied policy of records retention ended up destroying the company. Congress has also enacted laws since Andersen that require

Shredding electronic data.

LESSON LEARNED:

> Just as with conventional documents and discovery,
> signs of intentional destruction or attempts at hiding
> evidence will not reflect favorably on your case.
> Document retention and destruction policies must
> be implemented under neutral conditions and
> consistently followed to prove "reasonable efforts"
> and to avoid hints of obstruction. Picking and
> choosing what to retain and what to destroy is not a
> records retention policy! Be aware that the programs
> you use can be evidence in and of themselves. Do
> you really want to have your witnesses explain using
> "Evidence Remover"?

In one case contested in federal court in Chicago, a company was punished
after its owner bought a copy of a software program called "Evidence
Eliminator" to erase files from his computer. The judge in the case threatened that the owner's suit against a rival over patent infringement be
thrown out because of the owner's "egregious conduct." The judge forced
the offender to pay a portion of his opponent's fees and costs.[14]

document retention in situations like those illustrated in the case. In 2002, Congress
enacted the Sarbanes-Oxley Act, partially in response to Andersen. Among other things,
the Act imposes various retention requirements on publicly traded companies and imposes
liability on their chief executive and financial officers for violation of such requirements.

[14] "Costly electronic discovery part of potentially every case in the 21st Century", Chicago
Tribune Online Edition, April 10, 2005

Moreover, even with wiping programs, forensics can look into nooks and crannies that wiping programs can miss. There will be evidence that the wiping program was installed, which will put your firm in a bad light, unless your firm's document retention policy specifies wiping and it is done on a regular basis well before your conversations with the Attorney General. Of course, even then, you need to stop wiping when you believe there is a lawsuit possible, and most certainly if you receive a preservation order or spoliation letter. Send out a stronger letter to mandate preservation activities. Make it clear no one is helping by deleting files. Audit and monitor compliance.

Inside Counsel

SCENARIO: **Your company has made headline news (for the wrong reasons)**

> *A workplace tragedy has occurred, and your friends and executive management are in the hot seat. The government is inquiring and your shareholders are suing; this can be a company-ending event. Suddenly, from all sides, you are being asked to counsel and respond to six different law firms, each handling a different aspect of this same matter. Your insurance company is paying to defend you and the counsel they have chosen needs access to your most sensitive data. How do you give them access to only the material they request, in a secure environment outside of your firewalls?*
>
> *The lawyers from all those different firms are monopolizing the people in IT who are responsible for keeping the business running. They are complaining that some lawyers want last year's email, some want this year's email and some want to send in a black bag collection team to forensically sweep the entire executive suite.*

LESSON LEARNED:

> Once you are in multiple litigations, identify key people involved in each one. Issues will change across cases, impacting responsiveness. You can gain a time advantage by reviewing material for both junk and privilege only once. This saves money and reduces risk of producing a privileged item in different litigation

and serves as a junk filter across multiple litigations. By planning ahead, having repeatable processes in place and reducing duplicative reviews, you can lower the costs of the collective litigations, create more favorable outcomes, minimize the impact of litigation on the people running your company, and benefit the company's bottom line.[15]

SCENARIO: **Getting ready for common matters**

Perhaps you are not faced with a crisis, as in the previous scenario. In fact, your days may be quiet, with nothing more shattering than the occasional employee leaving with company assets or disgruntled ex-employee threatening a suit. Is there a low cost way to protect and process the company for these everyday threats, without going overboard?

LESSON LEARNED:

First, make it policy to remove hard drives from all departing employees' machines with documentation to preserve chain of custody. Replace with a new drive and redeploy the equipment. Store the removed drive securely, perhaps offsite with a third party. If the departing employee sues, chances are there is something on the preserved drive that you can use during impeachment of testimony. Without the preserved drive, the ex-employee can testify you destroyed evidence favorable to them, meeting one of the Zubulake factors.

Relatively simple safeguards go a long way. Should a matter arise, obtaining the electronic evidence from the employee's own preserved machine is comparatively easy and low cost.

With records management in place you can develop a procedure to take the material from ex-employees hard drives, classify it and retain or dispose in accordance with your records retention policy and litigation holds.

---

[15] "Litigation Readiness: Mastering the Inevitable," by Tim Stevens and Prashant Dubey. 2004. Contact Fios for more information.

Get serious with IT.

SCENARIO: **Get serious with IT**

> *Imagine that you and the CIO have never gotten along —
> especially, you feel, she's never understood the legal ramifications
> of her IT policies nor paid attention to your requests. Recently,
> you sent her a preservation letter for a matter. Now you and her
> top email administrator are sitting at the deposition table. He is
> answering the question, "What is your email retention policy?"
> with the business-as-usual answer of "30 days." You trust that
> he will surely go on to explain that he received a preservation
> letter causing him to suspend that policy for this matter. He is
> asked, "Is that policy still in place today?" Your heart begins
> pounding in your ears as you take in the implication of his
> answer, "Yes." You call for a recess. Sure, the CIO forwarded
> your preservation letter to the email administrator. (You have a
> vague recollection of hearing about upgrading the email system
> and IT being shorthanded...) Obviously, the importance of
> your request was not understood by the email administrator, nor
> did the CIO follow up to enforce it.*

LESSON LEARNED:

> Get written verification that your orders to IT are being
> taken seriously. Ask about the who's and how's of getting
> preservation done. You may be able to assist IT in getting
> supplemental funds for the new tapes and resources they
> need to comply. Have frequent informal conversations
> and engender an atmosphere of trust and partnership.

Increasingly, the courts are holding counsel more responsible for assuring that preservation duties and destruction holds are enforced. For example, the Zubulake case discusses counsel's preservation obligation: — "Counsel must oversee compliance with the litigation hold, monitoring the party's efforts to retain and produce the relevant documents." — "[I]t is not sufficient to notify all employees of a litigation hold and expect that the party will then retain and produce all relevant information." Judge Scheindlin put the obligation on inside and outside counsel to monitor the preservation effort.

SCENARIO: **Know what's possible and keep tabs on outside counsel**

Your company is in a class action. Your outside counsel sent "form responses" back to the plaintiffs denying any electronic documents existed (read: they don't understand electronic discovery). Not amused, the judge ordered your company to produce and, just for good measure, ordered your company not to delete any data from "anywhere." Your CIO tells you there are batch processes which empty out transaction files, meaning that programming will be necessary to keep them intact per the order.

Meanwhile, emails are piling up and IT is afraid to load balance the servers because they do not want to run afoul of the judge's preservation order. Your outside counsel says they will help you get the order overturned but it will take 4 months, more time than your business has to make sure the infrastructure does not keel over.

You've always wanted a seat at the executive table, and now you may get the chance because you can safeguard the company from such risks in the future. You are beginning to understand both law and technology, and will be sure to reach out to an expert 3rd party for help (and be monitoring your outside counsel for their electronic discovery savvy from now on).

LESSON LEARNED:

> Especially in the early part of a class action, monitor the responses of your outside counsel so you do not end up backed into a corner. Plan for a long siege. Partner with your IT department; you will need favors from them and their actions can make or break your credibility in your case. Because class actions have a local component you will need someone who can gain communication deep into a corporate IT structure.

Outside Counsel

Even if you consider yourself well informed about electronic discovery, you'll want to reduce your exposure by keeping an eye on electronic discovery partners and vendors — including outside counsel — and by staying in charge of the high-level decision making.

Consider the case of financier Ron Perelman vs. Morgan Stanley. Headline: "Morgan Stanley to Fire Law Firm," Morgan Stanley, vilified by a state court judge for failing to produce documents in a high-profile legal fight with financier Ronald Perelman, is moving to replace its main law firm in the case . . . The Wall Street brokerage house said it has become clear that the court "has lost all confidence in any statement or representation made" by lawyers at Kirkland and Ellis LLP., and that Morgan Stanley has put the firm . . . On notice 'of a potential malpractice claim" arising out if its representation."Wall Street Journal — March 23, 2005

Know what's possible, keep tabs on vendors.

SCENARIO: **Choose higher level partners**

> *Your electronic discovery vendor has just informed you that they cannot get data off key backup tapes. You trust them, and bring that information to court. The court orders the tapes to be given to the opposition. To your embarrassment, the opposition's expert restores them in a few days and finds responsive data.*[16]

LESSON LEARNED:

> Verify claims of impossibility with other vendors. Be careful to allow enough time to obtain second opinions. Waiting until a week before the discovery cutoff date will put your back to the wall. Choose a reliable electronic discovery partner — not just a junior-level vendor — with a proven track record of success, sophistication, and history of dealing with diverse challenges.

SCENARIO: **Don't assume your firm should host the data**

> *Your local counsel in a class action wants access to the data involved in your client's case. You are currently reviewing the data in house. Your internal IT has just told you it will take at least two months to procure and install the equipment and processes necessary to allow another firm access to the law firm's network.*

LESSON LEARNED:

> Consider who will need to access the data before choosing where to host it. Consider using 3rd parties, such as electronic discovery experts and vendors, to minimize impact on your firm's systems and daily business, and to maintain the ability to respond quickly to review requests. Issues of client confidentiality, office security, chain of custody, preservation of metadata and accessibility usually make your own law firm the least favorable place to host the data.[17]

---

[16] Residential Funding Corp. v. DeGeorge Financial Corp. 306 F. 3d 99 (2nd Cir. 2002)

[17] "Essentials of Electronic Discovery: Finding and Using Cyber Evidence," by Joan E. Feldman, Glasser LegalWorks, 2003.

CIOs and IT Directors

CIOs and IT directors are usually the last to know that they hold respon-sibility and culpability for producing evidence-quality data to meet the demands of their outside counsel. Many corporations segregate discus-sions on sensitive legal matters to those who "need to know." Outside counsel often procrastinates in determining an electronic discovery approach, hoping a case will settle or they can negotiate a "gentleman's agreement" not to request electronic data.

Suddenly, back to the wall, the outside counsel will alarm the inside counsel with an impending deadline. Suddenly the CIO and/or IT director is under the spotlight to keep the opposition at bay with a quick production of electronic data.

It is imperative to know who among your team you can trust to deliver and to work well with the special communication challenges with the attorneys.

SCENARIO: **Mergers and acquisitions**

Your company is about to merge with another. You are notified that your attorneys need to review 5 years of data for 8 departments, 3 locations and 80 people. The data needs to be at the attorney's office next week. There is no court deadline, but the deal needs to close in the next 45 days or the terms change. Delay will subtract $20 million from the bottom line, as the price is tied to stock prices at a particular point in time. You look at your staff allocation and see that the IT key personnel are out on vacation and their designees are consumed with fighting fires to keep the operation running.

LESSON LEARNED:

Train your emergency response team in the proper way to collect evidence and have a 3rd party partner on deck who can be trusted to meet your needs in such a situation before it occurs.

Unhappy departure of a company president.

SCENARIO: **Unhappy departure of a company president**

Attorneys for an ousted president are asking for electronic data from his old computer. However, because IT budgets were so tight, all spare computers were routinely redeployed. The computer belonging to the departed president was returned "broken," and was sent back to the manufacturer for new hardware and an operating system upgrade. Data was overwritten in the process, and for data that survived, it's more difficult to prove chain of custody. Despite all this, a forensic expert was able to recover 3rd party emails and deleted commission files. This evidence caused a favorable settlement for the company.

LESSON LEARNED:

Don't be penny-wise and pound-foolish when it comes to IT policies, such as reuse of computers without preserving hard drives. This can complicate electronic discovery further down the road. If you do need to recover data, rely on experts to obtain it correctly to maintain its integrity and credibility. Also, train your employees that short of running the computer over with a car, deleted data can come back to haunt them.

Litigation Support

Many times, the electronic buck stops with the staff responsible for litigation support. This can be risky, especially if your attorneys are unfamiliar with the differences between hard copy and digital review, and when you don't fully comprehend the pitfalls of gathering electronic data yourself.

SCENARIO: **Luddite in a hurry**

> *Your attorneys have a case that involves a lot of electronic data. But they are so computer phobic, they don't even answer their own email. They have no idea what they're in for. A partner naively asks you to print out the 50 CDs worth of data (which have been gathering dust on his desk for the last two weeks) so he can review it "over the weekend at home." He doesn't realize you will need a moving van to ship the boxes of paper he's asked to review. Now you are frantically calling print vendors to assist you on the Friday before Memorial Day, hoping to have something for him to review on Saturday.*

Luddite in a hurry.

LESSON LEARNED:

> Know your limitations (and theirs) and get expert help. Electronic data is different from paper documentation and is more voluminous than some attorneys imagine. Plan ahead, and make sure your attorneys are educated as well.

SCENARIO: **In-house review**

> *Your firm expects you to go out and collect the client's data. You have a modicum of computer knowledge (probably more than the attorneys do!), so you confidently go to the site and begin interviewing witnesses. The witnesses point out key documents, which you burn to CDs. You bring the CDs back to the law firm and dump them on a big server. But it's not that easy. After cleaning up the virus attack you've picked up from the client's files, and apologizing to the firm's other clients for the spam war it launched, your firm's IT department finally gives you offline resources to do reviews.*

LESSON LEARNED:

> Don't assume you know how to collect electronic evidence correctly for legal purposes. Be careful of reviewing client data on your own machines. Take precautions, such as working off of copies, virus scanning and using machines isolated from your network.

SCENARIO: **Selective review at the client site**

> *You click around and open a few documents at the desktop of each witness to make sure they are responsive and not privileged and burn a CD to bring back to the office. You copy the many CDs to your law firm server and use standard Windows search tools to determine relevance and potential privilege. You print the documents for the attorneys to review.*
>
> *At trial, the key piece of evidence is now in question because the "Create Date" comes later than the "Modified Date" because you didn't understand how to extract and protect a native file — you merely copied files from one device to another, altering metadata and chain of custody all the way. Your firm is now being sued for malpractice because it appears that an agent of the firm, you, has altered key evidence.*

> *Inside the file, when it is looked at forensically, your name appears. That's how they know you are involved.*
>
> *Only later on, during your experience on the stand, do you learn that CDs have a different operating system, overstamping key dates with the date of collection. You learn that opening up Microsoft Office documents on your computer can cause your name to be embedded in the document even if you are careful about closing the document without saving. Autosave features can get you in trouble too, by muddling metadata.*

LESSON LEARNED:

> Have a 3rd party expert collect relevant data using collection procedures appropriate to the level evidence demands. Preserve native files so it is possible to produce from the unaltered file and protect the admissibility of the evidence. Rarely can in-house litigation support staff manage all aspects of electronic data collection correctly or quickly. Communicate to the partners, where appropriate, how their requests to you are different when they involve electronic data.

Hopefully these war stories entertained and gave you some useful background and lessons from the real world.

But remember, despite the potential complexities of individual cases and scenarios, the key steps of electronic discovery remain the same, regardless of the specifics of the litigation or investigation:

1. Strategy
2. Collection
3. Processing
4. Review
5. Production

These steps provide the framework for the process you will follow to help reduce risk and maximize benefits from electronic discovery. During each step, there are specific activities that can further solidify your position if followed properly. Some are simply good practice, such as researching the opposition, anticipating requests, and developing a defense. Others are mandatory and specific to electronic data, such as collecting and preparing electronic evidence.

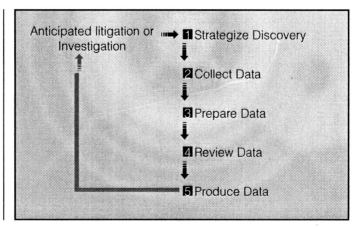

Successful electronic discovery starts with strategy development and negotiation with the opposition. Done early on, this sets the scope of discovery and establishes the preservation responsibility. From there, you can proceed through a methodical progression of data collection, processing, review and production.

4

WHY IS ELECTRONIC DISCOVERY SO IMPORTANT?

A number of drivers are creating a dramatic increase in the use of electronic discovery services.

The most significant is the explosive growth in electronic data. According to recent estimates published in Law Technology News, at least 93% of business documents are created electronically, and more than 35% of corporate communications never reach paper.[18]

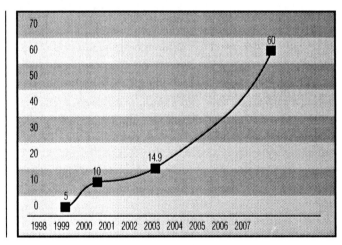

Source: "How Much Information? 2003" by UC Berkeley's School of Information Management and Systems. October 27, 2003.
http://www.sims.berkeley.edu/research/projects/ how-much-info 2003/internet.htm

---

[18]Source: "How Much Information? 2003" by UC Berkeley's School of Information Management and Systems. October 27, 2003. http://www.sims.berkeley.edu/ research/projects/how-much-info 2003/internet.htm

The prevalence of email as a primary form of corporate communication adds to the enormity of electronic documents in use today. For example, the School of Information Management and Systems (SIMS) at the University of California, Berkeley, states daily email traffic is expected to almost double by 2006, from 31 billion messages today to 60 billion messages.[19] Other sources say that while many people send and receive fewer than 10 emails a day, others exceed 40 a day.[20]

Another key driver is the widespread need for risk management in today's economy. The heightened scrutiny of corporate activity translates into a corresponding increase in the liability exposure of CEO, president, CFO and other "CXO" positions. This exposure is frequently linked to electronic corporate communications such as email and associated file attachments. In regulated industries, earning compliance and avoiding penalties also hinges upon electronic discovery and data audit trails.

Finally, as electronic documents and emails become ubiquitous, how a corporation routinely stores or destroys such data becomes increasingly important to potential future litigation, because the need for prompt and thorough access to electronic documents is crucial. A poorly thought out records management policy can result in overly burdensome and costly responses to discovery, missed evidence, and lost metadata that may have impacted litigation for one party or the other. Thus, electronic discovery and how to anticipate it and respond to it are increasingly important to corporations.

Can Electronic Discovery Ever Be Ignored?

According to legal cyber expert Joan A. Feldman, "what you don't know can hurt you."[21] This is especially true because fewer and fewer documents ever make it to hard copy. Today, electronic data — not paper — reveals the complete story.

---

[19] Ibid., Since 1995, e-mail volume has increased, though sources differ as to the degree of the increase. A study by Rogen International and Goldhaber Research Associates found that in 1995, employees sent an average of only three e-mails a day and received five. By 2002, employees were sending an average of 20 a day and receiving 30. A 1999 study reported in Newsweek estimated that "a white-collar worker" receives about 40 e-mail messages in the office every day. Anecdotally, one of the contributors to this Guide receives an average of 3,000 e-mails a month.

[20] Ibid.

[21] *"Essentials of Electronic Discovery: Finding and Using Cyber Evidence,"* by Joan E. Feldman, Glasser LegalWorks, 2003.

The limitations of paper-based document review become a harsh reality when compared against the sheer mass of electronic information created in corporate settings. It is virtually impossible to print out, organize and review every electronic document, email or digital voice mail using the traditional processes for paper review.

Moreover, for those familiar with electronic discovery, it is clear that electronic content and audit trails reveal much more than their paper counterparts. An electronic file contains easily accessible and highly reliable corporate knowledge, leaves a metadata chronology of key dates, comments between collaborators and, in effect, a knowledge map of who knew what, and when it became known.

Ignoring electronic forms of evidence — or not knowing how to find, preserve and produce those that are relevant — can seriously limit your litigation effectiveness.

How Is Electronic Discovery Different?

The good news and the bad news is that digital data is rarely ever 'gone' even if a party believes they have deleted a file. Thus it can be discovered. However, specialists in forensic computing are needed to retrieve the data while preserving its metadata and enabling the evidence to stand up in court.

Copying files from one device to another for 'review' opens the door to an authenticity challenge for key evidence.

In addition, because electronic data can be exchanged, copied, forwarded, and modified so freely by individuals other than the original owner, demonstrating the chain of custody becomes a crucial issue.

How electronic data is stored — as active files or as backup tapes, on desktop computers or on mobile devices, on servers or handhelds — affects the procedures and costs involved in retrieving evidence. It's not as straightforward as requesting "all emails" or asking for old-fashioned banker's boxes stuffed with memos.

Then there are technical issues. Review databases differ in how they organize data — can the system you are considering match the fields and scale to receive the data provided by a respondent? Can it accept electronic documents in a variety of formats? Does data "flow" into a format that can be readily culled, reviewed, protected for privilege and categorized? We'll go into these and other technical issues later, as well describe how to prepare for electronic discovery.

In a nutshell, while electronic evidence is fair game for discovery, the traditional, paper-based discovery procedures do not readily translate to the digital paradigm."[22]

The process of electronic discovery may seem overwhelming, but as we've shown, there are significant legal risks if you try to avoid the process altogether. Navigating the seemingly complex maze of the electronic discovery process does not have to be difficult. Nor is it recommended or even possible for any but the few firms with an expert electronic discovery practice to do it all alone — any more than you would be expected to forego the use of other experts, such as financial forensics or expert witnesses, to make your case. Electronic discovery can be manageable when you are familiar with the process and if you select the right partner.

In addition, when electronic evidence is managed, from creation, with a document management system — the Evidence Management Lifecycle — the entire process becomes faster, automated and repeatable without redundancy.

---

[22]"Disinterring the Inaccessible and Intangible; The Fundamental Challenge of Electronic Discovery," by Dean Gonsowski, J.D., C.I.S.S.P. *Trial Talk*, August/September 2003.

5

HOW TO GAIN A STRATEGIC ADVANTAGE

Just as individuals are affected in varying ways by electronic discovery, so too do specific legal areas have special concerns. The following sums up the strategies that can help bolster your position, depending on the kind of matter and what your area of responsibility might be.

Class Actions

Class actions generally start out in state courts where electronic evidence is not very well understood by the judge. Plaintiff's attorneys are deposing the IT department of their target early in the process to get the target on record as destroying evidence in the normal course of business. It is important to play your best game from the beginning.

- **Do not appear to have something to hide.** For example, continuing with "standard policy" 30-60 day cutoffs on email retention or overwriting tape backups can be perceived as deliberately destroying evidence. Once litigation becomes a possibility (yes, determining what you knew and when you knew it can be dicey), the preservation obligation kicks in. Claiming ignorance simply doesn't work with electronic data, as shown in the Morgan Stanley case brought by financier Ron Perelman.[23]

---

[23] After several egregious examples of playing "hide the evidence," Morgan Stanley was ruled to be "grossly negligent" in turning over documents... Destroying some emails and assuring the court that everything had been handed over when it hadn't. The judge took the unusual step of saying Morgan Stanley would have to prove to a jury that it didn't help Sunbeam defraud Mr. Perelman. Typically the burden of proving fraudulent behavior lies with the plaintiff. (Wall Street Journal, March 5, 2005).

- **Consider the jurisdiction.** Forum shopping by plaintiffs looking for the most advantageous venue may find you in court with a judge who knows nothing about electronic data. Find an electronic evidence partner with experts who can speak plain language rather than jargon to the judge, and who can assist you in tailoring your motions to meet the needs of the specific jurisdiction. Even though the Class Action Fairness Act[24] will bring most electronic discovery under Federal Rules, pre-certification discovery can still impact at the state level.

- **Make sure you are up on federal, state and local rules.** Do not expect all federal courts to follow one standard. Get familiar with the local rules. Delaware, New Jersey and New York have some interesting twists of process for electronic discovery. See **www.kenwithers.com** for up to date rules of the road.

- **Prepare for varying data collection requirements.** Until the class action is certified or removed, you will have special data collection requirements by state. Identify and track your custodians by department, project and state from the beginning as there may be state issues even in a case removed to federal court.[25]

- **Plan for the long run.** Class actions drag on. In anticipation, always have in place a data retention plan for departed employees.

- **Reduce redundancy** and multiple response strategies. Identify your core custodians early for the class action. Collect them once and produce them often.

- **Use conceptual analysis** to identify keywords. Measure the impact of keywords prior to negotiating them.

- **Establish regular collection windows** for easier tracking and less impact on the client's IT department. This is necessary because class action reviews tend to expand. You may need to refresh the collection the next year and you'll want to direct the collection team to collect only new data.

---

[24]Class Action Fairness Reform Act of 2005. (CAFA)

[25]Ibid.

- **Meet regularly with the IT department and records managers.** Assess who will make the best witness at the deposition. This may not be the email administrator (who can provide hair-raising details of how email is lost on a regular basis). Instead, you may want the highest level person to be deposed, with the preparation for the deposition facilitated by outside counsel or consulting experts. Make sure your witnesses are shielded from strategy discussions.

- **Track what has been produced to each requesting party.** Make sure you produce the same thing to other parties. Don't try to hold back. There are websites selling CDs full of produced evidence, protective orders or not. Inadvertently holding something back in one jurisdiction can impact your case nationally. Make sure your protective orders have teeth to reduce evidence sharing.

- **Limit unnecessary multiple or redundant reviews.** You will probably be working with many outside counsel. Make sure there is only one privilege review for each custodian. Producing a privileged item in one jurisdiction may cause you to lose the privilege in another jurisdiction.

- **Stay flexible and engage a partner.** Find an experienced electronic discovery partner with flexible production options. You will need to produce to a multitude of different law firms, each with their own software to review your production. At some point, lead counsel will be appointed and a general repository for all law firms will be established. Consider controlling the choice of that repository yourself.

Second Requests

By their very nature, second requests are on a short deadline and put you in a defensive position. Corporations that are of a certain size who intend to merge or spin off must, by law, file information with the appropriate government agency, usually the Department of Justice or Federal Trade Commission. This is the silent "first request." The governmental agency has a certain number of days (generally 30) to determine if they need more information to green light the transaction. This is when the "Second Request" appears.

The agency generally uses the same boiler plate over and over with a few additions. This forms the foundation for negotiations to begin narrowing the scope of the request. They generally make a "kitchen sink" request that can be dramatically narrowed by knowledgeable and experienced counsel. There is usually no time to go it alone unless you have a lot of electronic experience and the dedicated resources to pull it off. So, be proactive in anticipation of the worst. For most of us, second requests mean:

- **Before the deal is done, choose an electronic discovery partner.** Make up a mock case and send a non-involved low-level custodian's email box to the vendor as a sample, so as not to expose your pending merger. Train your discovery team in the review tool you will use in your second request. Establish the data flow to and from your potential partner. Keep your strategy safe and in your pocket by doing this early.

- **Do not wait for the 2nd request to begin collecting data.** Of course, you will want to argue burden, cost and reasonableness in your negotiations. However, desktops take time to collect. Identify your key custodians and begin collecting the desktops anyway. Remember that executives with laptops need a convenient time to have data collected from them.

- **Read the request carefully.** Some recent requests required "create and access" dates to be maintained as metadata, which impacts how data is to be collected. Unless that requirement was negotiated away, it mandated evidence quality collection methods rather than simple drag and drop. Consider early collection using evidence quality protocols to make this a non-issue. Ask your e-discovery partner for a project plan which works backward from your desired production date. Estimate volumes and pages/reviewer to determine what level of bulk categorization, duplicate review and incorporation of conceptual strategy meets your time and substantial compliance needs.

- **Negotiate what to produce first.** Active data is the fastest to collect and therefore to review. Negotiate a protocol which has desktops and laptops as a secondary production (and archived data as a very distant third). You may be able to narrow the scope of custodians and date ranges by then.

- **Get a critical mass of custodian data in a review tool to allow concept searching.** Concept searching will go beyond keyword searching, and even generate appropriate keywords, all to help minimize effort while maximizing potentially responsive results. Test the keywords for substantial compliance. Use the keywords in negotiations and/or to demonstrate that the time period is too broad. Demonstrate your "substantial compliance."

- **Negotiate the form of production early.** Waiting until the end can add days to the production date. Printing to hard copy, for example, can delay your compliance by days. With paper bound regulators, some second request participants have negotiated the electronic data first, while maintaining the option of dealing with the paper later. They rarely choose paper. Do not assume your agency will love the idea of your producing native files as they will need to do something with the files before reviewing them.

- **Negotiate clear guidelines on what is considered fair game.** For example, chat (instant messages) is not normally collected. Some chat, however, is being retained by financial firms. Chat can be recorded by opponents to your transaction. Take a measure and determine the importance of chat. Other evidence sources that should be negotiated include 3rd party email (like Yahoo and Hotmail), home computers, Personal Digital Assistants (PDAs), and cell phones. It is usually the quasi-criminal agencies that are interested in these items, not the FTC, SEC or DOJ looking for substantial compliance for a commercial transaction.

- **Inventory your backups. Know what you have and be able to prove it and produce it.** This can be accomplished by either a physical inventory or an electronic catalog, which is much less expensive than a full restore of each tape. Negotiate that tape (archival) data be produced last. As productions and negotiations continue, concentrate on reducing the time period for which production is required. This will dramatically reduce restore and de-duplication charges. On the other hand, restoring, de-duplicating, reviewing and producing targeted archival (tape) data can make you appear extremely compliant and diligent.

- **Make sure your vendor and partner in electronic discovery has experience with second requests.** If they do not know what a "spec number" is, for example, take a pass. Spec number is short for specification number. The government has a standard template they use as the kitchen sink for second requests with each area designated by spec number. They used to demand production by spec number. Some recent cases have allowed production "in the course of business," which usually means by custodian or department, the way most data is collected.

Intellectual Property Disputes

There are two sides when litigation arises about intellectual property (IP), so we will delineate the perspective from the viewpoint of both sides of the dispute.

Your company has been accused of stealing secrets.

Your VP of Sales has been crowing about recruiting a key sales person from your fiercest competitor. He cleared the hiring with Human Resources around the issues of territory and non-compete. Now, the competitor has filed suit asking a court to allow their expert to inspect your entire network to satisfy themselves that your new hire did not purloin their confidential information.

- **Be prepared to prove a negative.** When hiring from a competitor, anticipate an accusation. Assess the risk with the help of counsel. Set aside the earliest backup tape you have outside of the regular rotation to establish your client list and product plans prior to hiring this individual. Preserve the data of the key departments.

- **Counsel the new hire** and his/her new coworkers regarding the conditions of hire. Conditions of hire that should be signed off on include not bringing in any client list, work product and any other confidential information or trade secret.

- **Train IT and put a procedure in place** to schedule any transfer of data from your new hire's machine to your company machine for a few days later than the request. Trigger a notification to inside counsel of the request and make sure they sign off before any transfer of data on to a new machine for the new hire. Make sure everyone — human resources, IT, the hiring group, and coworkers — understand the priority and need for these safeguards.

- **Isolate the new hire's backups.** While this is not the ideal position to be in, you can minimize risk by giving the new employee brand-spanking new equipment. Consider creating a separate backup media for the new hire until you are certain you will not be sued.

- **Check in periodically** with your new hire to make sure they are complying with their agreement.

- **Meet with opposing counsel and agree on a 3rd party neutral.** Many firms have found themselves in the predicament of trying to prove a negative. They are accused of having a client list, drawings, plans or budgets. The opposition will want to inspect your systems. Even if the firms involved in the dispute are not competitors, no company wants hostile parties combing through their live systems. Have the opponent provide a 3rd party expert with the files showing the intellectual property believed stolen. Allow the 3rd party neutral to collect an appropriate subset from your system. One case was settled on favorable terms when there were no file names in common. Another needed to digitally fingerprint each file (hash) for the accused and the accuser and do a comparison. Finding only one file in common, a shareware program, facilitated that settlement. Still others require experts to review both sets of documents looking for similarities beyond an exact copy.

You believe your ex-employee has taken company secrets to a competitor.

Now imagine the shoe is on the other foot. How can you process the legal landscape so you can prove, if you unfortunately have to, that an ex-employee has made off with intellectual property or confidential company information?

- **Make conditions of hire and continued employment clear and specific from the beginning.** Upon hire, have employees sign a statement that they are not allowed to bring other companies' IP into your company nor remove any from yours. Draw your non-compete, trade secret and confidentiality conditions narrowly. Specify penalties for non-compliance. Make sure there is a record of any home computer that may be used for work purposes.

- **Train managers in the art of firing people or facilitating a voluntary departure.** Make sure there is a culture of treating people fairly. Counsel people before firing them. Let the person go at the end of the day. As you are releasing the person, have IT document taking their equipment from their workstation.

- **Secure the recovered equipment so it is not quickly redeployed.** Have the network administrators take a snapshot of their home directories and email files. Instruct the email administrator to undelete any emails before the snapshot, a secret feature of leading enterprise email platforms. Ask the employee to bring in any material they brought home back to the human resources or legal office and to sign an exit statement that they no longer have any material, along with their original non-compete agreement attached. Explain and document your expectations that they will not carry material to their new employer and let them know you will be contacting the other company's counsel to reiterate that expectation.

- **Put the receiving company on notice.**

- **Forensically analyze the computers and all media recovered, just in case unsanctioned sharing activity has already commenced.**

- **Look for evidence of mass deletions.** This often indicates a server dump, most often burned to CD or emailed via 3rd party email to a home computer. A claim of a "broken computer" also indicates foul play, as does a reformatted hard drive. Data can be recovered from reformatted hard drives. It is important not to ask IT to just "look at the email and files" because by doing so they will affect the chain of custody record, triggering dates on files to appear as if they were accessed or changed after the employee left.

- **Consider special handling for production of source code.** If software code theft is at issue, consider the impact of producing the code electronically. It could be altered enough to not be a copyright violation, and then be recompiled. Newer programming platforms even allow source code to be migrated from language to language (such as from C to Visual Studio .NET), obviating copyright claims. Instead, consider making the source code available in a searchable review tool, without offering download or batch print capability. Producing to paper will force your opponent to scan it, putting it right back in electronic form. Consider engaging a software forensics expert who can read code in many languages to testify as to the similarities of the programs.

- **Analyze the print logs.** Developers, by the nature of their digital savvy, may think they can cover up the electronic trail of any theft. But consider this hypothetical scenario in which even they can be discovered: A hapless programmer is clever enough to not copy his code from his computer to a removable media or to email. Instead, he thinks he is covert to only print out a hardcopy of it. The evidence can still be traced via the company's print server logs, which record file names and the user who sent the print job.

You've received a production of electronic files

SCENARIO:

> *You've received a TB of native files as a result of a judge granting your motion to compel production in a form which can be digested by your firm within the bounds of the discovery cutoff date. What a victory to convince the judge that those 3 dumb terminals available 9 to 5 for a page by page review would require many thousands of days of review. Your attorneys slapped a searching tool on the server and started searching away, opening documents and emailing them back and forth amongst themselves. They've found electronic documents directly contradicting depositions. Your attorneys now want to introduce those documents into evidence, but the "modify" date on the file is after the date they produced to you.*

LESSON LEARNED:

When receiving native files, treat it as a forensic event. Image the media and keep an evidentiary copy. You may get lucky and the producing party may reuse media and your forensics could surface other items. Of course, if it surfaces privileged items, you may need to give them back under ethical rules or a clawback agreement, but it's fair game if it isn't criminal law where all the "fruits of the poison tree" are excluded from evidence. Once your evidence copy is made, search and review any way you want, but when it comes time for production, produce from the evidence copy. Make sure you have a hash of the file to produce with it.

If you are the producing party, make sure your production is "reasonable" and does not lend itself to being turned into an unfortunate event. Make sure you've reviewed for privilege. Remember, hidden columns and password protected files can be opened. Produce the native files, if necessary, on clean media, with a hash of the entire production and each file so you can authenticate evidence if entered. Number each file, as you would Bates each page of a production. Make sure your Evidence Management system records the production.

6

WHO PAYS FOR ELECTRONIC DISCOVERY?

Opportunities for Cost Shifting

One way that electronic discovery differs from traditional discovery is the sheer volume and, especially for archived data, the technical issues and costs involved in recovering data.

These differences have heightened court awareness and sensitivity to questions of what constitutes undue burden; i.e., what information is worth disinterring, and who should pay for its production?[26] If you are cognizant of the issues and are prepared, you can take advantage of cost shifting for electronic discovery.

The Sedona Principles crafted by the Working Group on Electronic Document Production address the issue of whether and when, given the volume and costs of electronic discovery, the requesting party is required to show why efforts are warranted, rather than the traditional practice of the responding party demonstrating undue burden[27]:

---

[26] *Zubulake v. UBS Warburg,* LLC, No. 02 Civ. 1243 (SAS) (S.D.N.Y. May 13, 2003)

[27] *The Sedona Principles: Best Practices Recommendations & Principles for Addressing Electronic Document Production.* A Project of the October 2002 Sedona Conference Working Group on Best Practices for Electronic Document Retention & Production, March 2003.

Principle 5: "The obligation to preserve electronic data and documents requires reasonable and good faith efforts to retain information that may be relevant to pending or threatened litigation. However, it is unreasonable to expect parties to take every conceivable step to preserve all potentially relevant data."

Principle 7: "When the responding party has shown that it has acted reasonably to preserve and produce relevant electronic data and documents, the burden should be on the requesting party to show that additional efforts are warranted under the circumstances of the case."

Discussion continues about if and how the unique nature of electronic discovery, especially of legacy data, warrants changes in the Federal Rules of Civil Procedure, particularly Rule 26. Currently, the draft that looks like it will be approved by the Supreme Court and implemented in 2006 allows a safe harbor for "…the normal activity of an information system" … "absent exceptional circumstances" when data is erased inadvertently.[28]

Recent case law supports protection of responding parties from undue burden, if they have made reasonable and good faith efforts to preserve data.[29] These evolving opinions create opportunities for cost shifting if you are aware of how to manage your litigation readiness for electronic discover requests. Conversely, if you are the requesting party, your understanding of what constitutes good practice in electronic discovery and how to most effectively acquire the relevant data, can help minimize costs and protect against undue burden motions by the opposition.

How to Position for Optimal Cost Shifting

When it comes to who bears the cost burden of electronic discovery, there is a difference between accessible and inaccessible data.

Accessible data (also known as active or live data) means the documents are available without resorting to costly and time-consuming retrieval opera-

---

[28] See Ken Withers article, "Proposed Amendments to the Federal Rules of Civil Procedure," which shows the proposed changes as of May 11, 2005. *http://www.discoveryresources.org/pdfFiles/completeRules_051105.pdf*

[29] "Observations on The Sedona Principles," by John L. Carroll, Dean, Cumberland School of Law, Stanford University, Birmingham A; and Kenneth J. Withers, Research Associate, Federal Judicial Center, Washington DC.

tions. Accessible data could reside on servers, desktops, PDAs, optical disks, etc. Because the perception is that no undue efforts are required to make the data available, the producing party pays automatically, unless the request is overbroad.[30]

In contrast, inaccessible data (also known as archival data) or hidden data (for example, "deleted" files) require special tools and/or the services of forensic experts to be restored. Here, arguments can be made that the requesting party pays.

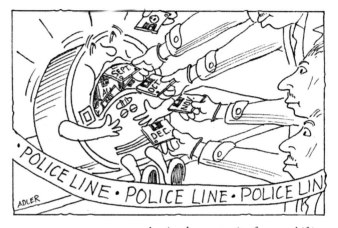

A missed opportunity for cost shifting.

SCENARIO: **A missed opportunity for cost shifting.**

> *A Fortune 100 company, knowing they had a potential government investigation looming, requested that their IT security team preserve data for them. Experienced users of EnCase,[31] the IT security team collected desktops in a forensic fashion and in an "active" (i.e., "live") fashion. As we'll see, active data cannot be shielded easily with arguments of undue burden, whereas archived data may be.*

---

[30] From *http://discoveryresources.blogspot.com.* "Many processes and strategies translated seamlessly from the paper world to the electronic world. Overbroad discovery requests did not."

[31] A forensics tool made by Guidance Software *(www.guidancesoftware.com).*

Next, anticipating that data for the past year would be requested, they restored a tape backup of data for each of the 12 months, without overwriting or de-duplication. This resulted in a total of 12 tape backups of highly duplicative data on a server, with each month in its own area of the disk. This effort was time consuming and costly and, while implemented with the best intentions of being litigation ready, actually undermined arguments for cost shifting. In fact, they had transformed inaccessible data into accessible data twice, first by proactively imaging the drives and next by turning the archival (tape) data into active (disk) data.

At last becoming concerned about the enormity of the data volume, the company asked for estimates and assistance in reducing the vast data set and about cost shifting. Unfortunately, they had already lost their opportunity to cost shift because they restored the archival data, on their own volition, before being compelled by discovery.

LESSON LEARNED:

All parties would have been better served by negotiating the scope and relevance of any digital data beforehand. This is because courts are increasingly willing to look to a sampling approach to determine whether to restore all or part of a tape library. Courts are beginning to see tapes as a disaster recovery tool that happens to be caught in litigation, not as reasonable preservation of active data. It is possible that the parties could have negotiated that one month's backups be restored for a small set of custodians. That data could have been reviewed and the responsive material produced at less than 10 percent of the cost otherwise incurred. The discussions between inside counsel and outside counsel about what to do with the newly restored data approached $100,000. Once an electronic discovery partner was engaged, de-duplication and other mitigation strategies were employed to reduce the review and production costs.

It's always a judgment call about what to collect in a forensic manner. In this case, the client had in-house resources so the collection was not overly expensive. They still have an argument to shift the costs for the analysis of the material. The risks and cost of managing electronic discovery in a crisis mode can be mitigated by education and training, so that legal and IT departments can mitigate the risks of managing a lawsuit in a crisis.[32] It is important for the legal and IT teams to begin to communicate as soon as possible, as technology decisions can impact the cost of responding to potential litigation.

A Strategy for Maximizing Cost Shifting

Courts are not amused by overbroad discovery requests, such as requiring parties to preserve "all" electronic documents or "all" email.[33] Thus, with preparation and foresight, you can maximize your opportunities for cost shifting and burden if you are faced with such a request. Jurists are increasingly looking toward the "reasonableness" of the request [FRCP 26 (b) (2)]. The following tactics can help build the case.

1. **Inventory.** Know how many and what kind of tapes you have. This will allow you to get estimates for restoring and de-duplicating the tapes. You can then submit those estimates with your arguments to demonstrate burden.

2. **Sample.** If the opponent has requested a four-year period, then four time slices may be appropriate for sampling. De-duplicate and review the material on those tapes to demonstrate that there is no responsive material on the tapes. Sample first and review the results before offering it to the requesting party. Know the impact of what you are offering.

---

[32] "Taming the Litigation Beast" by Mary Mack, Esq., *www.fiosinc.com/articles.html*, April 2004

[33] *http://discoveryresources.blogspot.com.* Ibid. As reported by Alexander H. Lubarsky, "a California Court did not only refuse to compel the Defendant to comply... but they fined the requesting party for its overbroad discovery demands." Posted Saturday, December 20, 2003.

3. **Select.** If you have chosen to preserve forensically, preserve broadly and analyze selectively the drives of individuals whom you believe will help your case. Not preserving material that could help your opponent could also prevent you from introducing material that will help your case.

4. **Wait.** You don't have to restore backup tapes just because you have them.[34] Wait until the opponent puts into evidence credible testimony that there is material on the tapes that will impact favorably on their case. The new Federal Rules which are slated to go into effect in 2006 recognize backups for disaster recovery rather than a deep cache for litigation. If the opponent requests forensic preservation or production, get an estimate to assist in burden shifting.

One benefit of the evolution toward a lifecycle of evidence management, enabled by document management systems and records retention policies, is that it becomes easier to capture and preserve potential evidence — as it is being created — rather than reactively searching and restoring archives.

---

[34]Creating backups is a relatively inexpensive activity. Therefore organizations are likely to do so. Restoring years of backups when faced with litigation is the costly part.

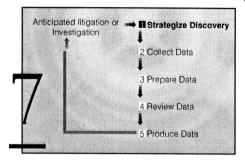

ELECTRONIC DISCOVERY
STRATEGY

Clouds gather and the winds have picked up, a storm may be forming on the horizon. Now's the time to be proactive and plan what, from an electronic perspective, you need to protect and process.

Consider your business objectives. For example, is speed more important than completeness? Do you need to over-comply because of past sanctions? What is the exposure? Have you conducted a risk/reward analysis? What is your budget for electronic discovery?

Early preparation and a well-structured strategy will greatly simplify the process of electronic discovery. Knowing up front how to handle the quantity and variety of data you're targeting, the individuals within the company who are most important, and what timelines you'll encounter will save you time and money in the long run. Federal and many state rules underscore the importance of early negotiations with the opposition to define scope, terms, and protocols of the electronic discovery. Negotiation and early understanding between parties can reduce unnecessary haggling and motions to compel.

For comprehensive and up-to-date information on federal, state and local rules regarding electronic discovery, see **www.kenwithers.com.** Some jurisdictions require that you come prepared with system schemas, preservation plans and a designated e-discovery witness. Even if you are not required to do so, planning for this meeting can pay hundreds of thousands of dollars in dividends of reduced motion practice, review, preservation and production costs.

Time Expectations

The time required to comply with an electronic discovery request is highly dependent on the scope of subject matter deemed potentially relevant, the amount of data involved, and your desired output for final production. The following time segmentation is a rough estimate of the relative time requirements for strategy, data collection, processing, review, production and de-brief. Be certain that you allow sufficient time for each phase of activity, especially the document review stage. By anticipating and planning for the resources you'll need, such as staffing, hardware, connectivity and communication methods, you'll be able to significantly streamline the discovery process.

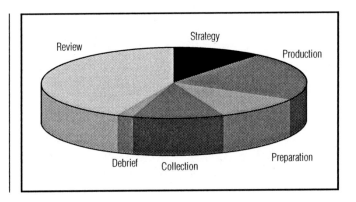

This chapter divides this first step into five sub-steps:

1. Evaluate the Preservation Obligation
2. Anticipate the Scope of Discovery
3. Research Opposition and Develop Offensive Strategy
4. Strategize the Discovery
5. Negotiate the Discovery

Preparing for Anticipated or Actual Proceedings

STEP ONE: Evaluate the Preservation Obligation

Understand the Data Universe

To understand your data universe, you must first identify your key IT and records management liaisons and start to establish a strong rapport. While it may not seem like you have the luxury to build relationships when faced with a production deadline, the payoff for hours invested here will be measured in days later. Your liaisons do not need to be the ones with all the technical information you need, as long as they know the people who do.

In a nutshell, you will need to evaluate the company's document retention and destruction policies and practice, communicate a preservation plan, and consider suspending document destruction and/or extending retention within appropriate areas of the company. Your electronic discovery partner should be able to supply templates and guidelines for creating and communicating a preservation plan.

Detailed tasks in this step include interviewing the Operations management responsible for data sources such as the CRM and ERP systems, and other applications and repositories such as collaborative document management repositories and enterprise content management systems. You will want to review IT documents and learn more about the company's data stores. You or your electronic discovery partner need to learn the company's various practices for data backup, restoration, decommission, upgrades and so forth. Now is the time to identify any selective destruction policies, quarantine key custodian data, and extend backup tape rotation.

Here's a checklist of what you need to find out from the company's document management team and IT managers.

1. **Document Retention Policy and Practice.** Discuss document retention policies and practices, with specific attention to document destruction. You may have to discuss retention practices with opposing counsel to minimize any surprises. Retention policies, even if they exist, are not always properly followed.

2. **Document Management System Structure.** Find out how the company's document management system, if one exists, is structured. These systems utilize software that labels content based on data source,

keywords and other parameters. You'll want to know how much total data is in the system, how old the data is and how much of it is potentially relevant to the specific matter. Additionally, you should identify any parameters that purge data based on content or time periods, as well as the frequency of backups. Standard retention and destruction policies should have been suspended for any potentially responsive data as soon as litigation seemed likely. A key word or conceptual search is one way to quickly identify and sequester likely candidates, and remove the need to 'save everything.' If you are using conceptual search, make sure you validate what is left behind via key word searches for defensibility purposes.

3. **Readiness to Produce Documents.** Determine the level of readiness to produce documents. How long will it take to identify and collect the live data and restore the relevant backup media, as well as review and produce relevant, non-privileged documents?

4. **Interrogatories and Depositions.** Identify those who have the greatest knowledge of the computer system. These individuals are likely targets for interrogatories and depositions.

5. **Exposure to Opposition Depositions.** Look for public information that could make other IT team members likely targets for the opposition. For example, it is often easy to find the names and contact information of technical managers on your client's website who may unintentionally disclose information about data retention or other policies.

6. **Designate a corporate witness** for electronic discovery issues who will not be involved in the day-to-day strategy discussions. You'll want your team to be able to speak freely without the possibility that the discussion will reappear in depositions or testimony.

TIP: Interrogatories and Depositions

A wealth of information can be targeted via electronic discovery interrogatories, requests for production and depositions. See the appendices of this guide for detailed suggested interrogatories, sample FRCP 30(b)(6) deposition questions, and requests for production.

Quickly Address Any Spoliation Issues

The term "spoliation" means the destruction or significant alteration of evidence, or the failure to preserve evidence, in pending, imminent or reasonably foreseeable legal proceedings. In such a situation, you may want to advise your client to avoid deleting or erasing information pursuant to their ordinary course of business. This is prudent even if such deletion was normal in the course of their standard business practices. A duty to preserve may arise when your client knows or should have reasonable knowledge that information is:

- The subject of a pending discovery request

- Reasonably likely to lead to the discovery of admissible evidence;

- Relevant to the anticipated or pending legal action; or

- Reasonably likely to be requested during discovery.

There are a variety of actions you can take to prevent spoliation, including the following:

- Identify any selective document destruction policies.

- Send out legal hold instructions to your client's information technology team. Schedule informational sessions with the team to explain the risks of spoliation and why the hold instructions are critically important.

- Suspend normal data destruction until further notice. Be sure, however, that a moratorium on destruction does not unnecessarily or adversely affect unrelated departments or areas of data storage. Also be sensitive to operating considerations, as computers need to be cleared of transaction data and logs in order to maintain peak performance.

- Send a spoliation letter to the opposition (see the appendices of this guide for a sample spoliation letter).

- Take "snapshots" (exact copies) of email boxes and other data stores of key individuals to maintain important evidence as well as data integrity and authenticity.

- Monitor compliance with the legal hold

- Offer a phone number for people to call with questions

- Reinforce the legal hold if your monitoring or phone calls indicate an issue

STEP TWO: **Anticipate Scope of Discovery**

Identifying and assessing the logical and reasonable criteria for the discovery will enable you to proactively manage the process of electronic discovery. The following five exercises will help you properly assess the potential scope of discovery:

1. **Determine the criteria for "Privilege" and "Relevancy."**
   - Determine what constitutes work product.
   - Consider ways to limit inadvertent waivers of privilege.
   - Start to assemble a list of privilege names, terms, and phrases to be used for proactively identifying potentially privileged documents.

2. **Determine the potential quantity of electronic data involved.**
   The amount of data involved affects many aspects of the project, including the method of collection and review, the number of reviewers needed, the time the project will take and how much it will cost. Work with the company's information technology staff to gain an understanding of the potential quantity of data that may need to be collected.

3. **Identify potential time and/or custodian slices.**
   Date range and custodian or "user" slices are the best ways to identify and rapidly cull (reduce) your data set so you won't unnecessarily collect too much data or perform inordinately large searches. Identifying these slices early in the process will also help you stay organized and reduce the likelihood that you'll conduct redundant searches at a later date.

4. **Review and negotiate the scope of discovery requests.**
   Review requests for production to help determine what data to target and collect. Negotiation for the scope of discovery is sometimes based on timeframes, custodians, and search terms and may be a way to help manage the size of the undertaking.

5. **Submit Voluntary Initial Disclosures if necessary.**
   The specific rules vary by jurisdiction. If Federal, you will need to list key custodians — Rule 26(a)(1)(A) — and produce or describe the documents — Rule 26(a)(1)(B).

1	**Determine the criteria** for "Privilege" and "Relevancy."
2	**Determine the potential** quantity of electronic data involved.
3	**Identify potential time,** custodian and/or user slices.
4	**Review and negotiate** the scope of discovery requests.
5	**Submit Voluntary Initial Disclosures** if necessary.

Ways to assess the scope of the project.

STEP THREE: **Research Opposition and Develop Offensive Strategy**

The goal of this step is learn as much as you can about your opponent. This includes the individuals or companies involved in the matter, as well as their counsel.

You need to understand opposing counsel's skills with regards to electronic discovery, and then formulate a strategy to exploit their weaknesses and solidify your strengths. It is essential to learn about their experience and prowess at handling electronic evidence in order to prepare for, if not pre-empt, their requests and motions.

Some of the questions you will want to answer:

• What type of experience has your opposition had with matters involving electronic discovery? Were they successful?

• Which electronic discovery vendors or partners have they used, and to what level of success?

• Do they consider themselves technically savvy? Do they market their ability to apply technology to their practice?

• How have they defined "electronic documents" in their discovery requests in past matters? If possible, try to get your hands on a request for discovery or production from one of their past matters.

What technology and software do they use internally to manage litigation?

Ask your electronic discovery partner for help. They should be able to provide some templates and guidelines, if not help with the actual research. Here are some creative tactics to learn more about the other side, specifically when preparing for a technical deposition:

- Send a test email with a made-up name to the company you are suing; for example, send an email to "xxxx@acme.com." It will likely bounce back with an "unknown recipient error", and when it does, the email headers will contain information about the IP addresses and alias names of the servers it passed through. Also, the bounced back message will indicate the type of email server and if you are lucky, whether they employ a content screener. If they do employ a content screener, it will be difficult for the opposition to cry "burden" when you want to retrieve emails by person, date and subject matter.

- Go to **www.whois.org** and enter the domain name of your opposition to learn the name of the main technical contact. This person will be a great target for finding out about infrastructure and backups. If they do not have the information themselves, they will know who has it.

- Search for resumes of people who were formerly employed by the opposition and contact them for information. Popular resume database sites include **www.careerbuilder.com, www.jobs.net, www.monster.com.**

- Look at the employment section of the opposition website in the targeted area. Under the skills and qualifications section, they will mention the type of software that is used. For basic operating system and office software, check executive clerical listings to find out if they are a Lotus Notes or Microsoft Exchange shop.

By the end of this step, you should be framing requests of the opposition and determining what data to target. If you haven't already, send a spoliation letter to the opposition if appropriate. Your opposition may voluntarily disclose important information, which can assist you in targeting your requests.

Review the interrogatories, requests for production (RFP), requests for admission (RFA) and determine what needs to be done to answer them.

STEP FOUR: **Strategize Discovery**

If you haven't done so already, select an electronic discovery vendor to partner with you. A qualified partner will be able to expedite the completion of the various discovery phases. The benefits of engaging professional help for electronic discovery are significantly greater if you involve the partner early in the discovery process. For example, a full-service electronic discovery partner can provide tools, templates, and other help to simplify your filings, evaluate the response burden using data sampling, provide cost extrapolations, and help reduce the overall amount of data to review and produce.

Armed with the information an experienced partner can provide, your discovery strategy may include seeking a protective order, requesting cost shifting (consider retaining an expert who understands the issues in electronic discovery), or proposals to the opposition to compromise or limit the scope of discovery. At this point, you should also decide how to handle requests for onsite discovery. An experienced partner, well-versed in the latest rulings and amendments to rules of civil procedure, can help you navigate the technical issues unique to onsite discovery.

It is always better to negotiate an agreement you can live with than to depend on the court to create one that will not harm the business. Supply suggested language and have information on costs and organizational impact at the ready if you find yourself in motion practice.

An early case assessment, where key custodians are collected and their data analyzed, can provide metrics to estimate costs. Conceptual searches can help generate keywords. Visual analytics on email communication can help scope the custodians likely to be impacted by this particular matter. Early case assessment, which includes electronic data, grounds settlement cost benefit analysis with objective and subjective evaluation. How do key custodians talk about the heart of the dispute?

For more information on cost shifting, see the "Who pays for electronic discovery?" chapter of this guide.

When to Outsource

There are a number of evaluation factors to consider before deciding to outsource your electronic discovery project. The following chart illustrates a number of situational criteria you'll want to assess prior to making your decision.

E-data as a percentage of all info (paper vs. e-data)	low % e-data	1 2 3 4 5 6 7 8 9 10	high % e-data
Financial exposure (risk)	low risk	1 2 3 4 5 6 7 8 9 10	high risk
Information volume	low volume	1 2 3 4 5 6 7 8 9 10	high volume
Timelines	long timelines	1 2 3 4 5 6 7 8 9 10	short timelines
Number of locations where data resides	few locations	1 2 3 4 5 6 7 8 9 10	many locations
People involved (custodians and witnesses)	few people	1 2 3 4 5 6 7 8 9 10	many people
Importance of data quality	not important	1 2 3 4 5 6 7 8 9 10	very important
Available internal resources (money and people)	significant resources	1 2 3 4 5 6 7 8 9 10	limited resources

Factors influencing electronic discovery outsourcing decision.

Partner Selection Criteria

The partner you engage for an electronic discovery project can significantly enhance or hinder your litigation management process. Spending a modest amount of time to gain a detailed understanding of each candidate's capabilities and track record will ensure that you select the most appropriate partner. There are a number of evaluation criteria to consider during the selection process. The following list provides a cross-section of consideration points to assist you in your decision.

- Talk with your colleagues and litigation support teams for initial recommendations on the most capable and reliable electronic discovery partners. Inquire how the partner handles the data collection, management and production challenges that are a normal course of litigation.

- Initial due diligence on your partner should include a review of their most complex electronic discovery projects and a detailed description of how they manage discovery projects from start to finish.

- Particularly for large projects, it is essential that you conduct site visits to the electronic discovery partners' facilities to gauge the level of sophistication, organization and security they offer for client projects.

- The partner needs in-depth expertise in rapidly identifying and collecting large quantities of data from multiple sources. Laptops, office desktops, home computers, PDAs, network servers, memory sticks, CD-ROMs, DVD-ROMS, backup tapes, other archive media and 3rd party storage and archival systems are all garden variety now. Make sure your partner can handle voice recordings, ECMs, records management system, remote collection and refresh collections.

- Be certain the partner has comprehensive procedures to establish and maintain a continuing chain of custody for sensitive electronic material, ensuring data security, accuracy and authentication.

- The partner, upon taking custody of your data, must be able to digitally fingerprint each file to ensure a legally defensible audit trail.

- The partner must identify documents not by extension but by state-of-the-art signature analysis. Because discovery strategies often require prioritizing the document types to review, knowing unequivocally the true file type distribution is critical.

- The partner must ensure that original data is never compromised by virus scanning all data to prevent cross-contamination.

- The partner should provide state-of-the-art security for data storage, including secure buildings, processing centers and employees. Firewall intrusion detection and protection, secure digital certificates, and a minimum of 512-bit SSL keys with 128-bit SSL encryption for any data transmissions are also extremely prudent.

- The partner's client services team should have in-depth legal experience and data engineers who understand the litigation process. You should request an introduction to the specific project manager who would be assigned to your account. Project managers should be able to manage projects spanning the lifecycle of the matter, not just reactive, spot productions.

- Make sure the partner isolates the experts you may need to testify for chain of custody purposes from the people helping you with your review strategy.

- Be certain that the partner is able to aggregate and convert electronic data into common formats such as HTML or TIFF, creating a unified and secure database of original content and metadata, fully indexed and optimized for searching.

- When it comes to the process of reviewing data, flexibility is of paramount importance. You should have the option to review data using the tool of your choice. Whether web-based review is selected, or any number of stand-alone litigation support review tools, the choice should be yours rather than be limited by a partner's capabilities or preferences.

- Because web-based (online) review is becoming the platform of choice for litigators, your partner should offer a web-based tool to enable your review team to work in any location that has Internet access, and to collaborate via secure instant messaging.

- For web-based data review tools, select a partner that offers a pricing model that allows unlimited usage and downloads for any number of users and for any length of online time. Avoid those that charge on a per-seat, per-document (i.e., per click) or per-hour license basis for data review to avoid delays for upgrading budgets.

- Since no file conversion technology can convert 100% of native files to a common review format such as HTML or TIFF, select a partner whose review tool supports quickly downloading copies of original documents in their native format. Further, the tool should support controlling who can download copies of original documents, and all downloads should be logged, enabling you to track who downloaded what material on specific dates.

- Your partner should enable you to identify the types of content to be included in the unified database via search parameters such as date ranges, custodians or data locations.

- Your partner should be able to help strategize and consult on search term filtering as a way to limit the discovery project. Identifying and filtering the right keywords and phrases is a critically important activity.

- Your partner's production standards should be impeccable. Output of selected electronic data must be produced quickly and delivered to your exact specifications. Flexibility is critically important. The partner should be able to produce selected documents in a wide variety of formats, including new web-based environments, PDFs, TIFF images with or without associated databases, native files, paper or any combination of these formats. Ask about quality control procedures on requirements as well as productions.

STEP FIVE: **Negotiate the Discovery**

Because the quantity of corporate electronic data is immense, it is important to limit electronic discovery to only that portion of the data universe that is potentially relevant to the proceeding. Sometimes the process of limiting discovery requires negotiation with opposing parties or court involvement. Your electronic discovery partner should be able to help you during these negotiations, especially regarding search terms that can affect the information you'd need to produce, as well as what evidentiary information you'll receive. Strategies can include:

- Meet with your opposition directly, or schedule and conduct a Rule 16 conference with a judge.[35]

- Define "electronic document" scope: active, archival, and/or forensic. (For a description of each, see the next chapter's Data Type table.)

- Determine which metadata fields are important to review.

- Agree on custodian and date range criteria

- Propose custodian and time slices.

- Propose location slices.

- Propose search terms such that all "hit" documents are either included or excluded from the review set (assuming you've assessed the impact).

---

[35]For more on the Federal Rules of Civil Procedure (FRCP), see *http://www.discoveryresources.org*. Proposed changes to the rules, many directly addressing the new issues raised by electronic evidence and discovery, are posted on this site as well.

- Negotiate a protocol for inadvertent disclosures.

- Define production.

- Negotiate a protective order.

TIP: Date Range Negotiations

If your client's data has already been collected, find out how it was collected prior to negotiating the date ranges for inclusion in the discovery set. Date range slices, if done without special collection tools, should be driven by the "last modified" date, as this date is typically the most reliable.

Specifying files dated after a given date introduces the risk of too many files being collected as part of your production, given that normal copy tools can change the "create" and "access" dates of files to that of the date of collection. Instead of leaving the range open (e.g., Jan. 2001 until now), specify an explicit endpoint (e.g., Jan. 2001 through Dec. 2003).

While it may seem like a small logistical detail, outlining your production requirements during this phase can also ensure more efficient production as you go forward. You'll want to evaluate the following production options:

- Determine your production format: paper, electronic data, or both. If electronic, decide between producing native files, images and text, images only, or a second web-based repository with limited review functionality.

- Determine if you'll need multiple production sets.

- Clarify delivery deadlines and locations.

- Clarify and agree on other production nuances, such as nomenclature, stamping, etc.

- Decide which subset of metadata fields you need to produce.

After you have taken the recommended steps to select your electronic discovery partner, establish your strategy, and define the production protocol, you're ready to take the second step: collect the actual data that you need to review.

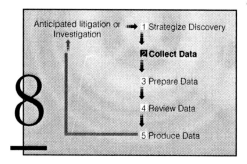

DATA COLLECTION:
MAINTAINING THE AUDIT TRAIL

By now the storm clouds are not just gathering, but the wind is blowing a gale, lightning strikes regularly, and you can feel the thunder. A legal proceeding — litigation or an investigation — is upon you. Yet, if you've completed at least some of the strategic steps outlined in the previous chapter, you are more than ready to weather the squall. The time has come to marshal the resources necessary to collect your data in a responsible, defensible manner.

For a thorough and efficient data collection you must conduct the following activities:

- Develop a collection plan

- Identify key contacts at your client's site(s)

- List all custodians and the location of their data

- Identify the sources of data (paper, active, archival, forensic)

- Decide who executes the collection

- Monitor the collection and chain of custody forms

A little later, we'll offer some factors to consider when deciding whether to collect on your own or engage an experienced partner.

Many businesses are diligent and organized about their electronic data storage and backup procedures, which will simplify collection. Yet, at many other companies, especially startups or the products of mergers and acquisition, data is not predictably stored or routinely preserved. You'll find that systematically archived and stored data is easier to access and can flow smoothly into a preservation system structured for legal purposes. Whether a company is diligent or lax about data storage and backup, transitory data (such as emails or documents kept on desktop computers) is always challenging to secure and gather. Fortunately, the complexities of collecting data can be easily managed by a competent electronic discovery services partner. One of the key areas of value offered by a partner is their experience with like customers, their understanding of what the bar for success looks like, and their ability to provide defensible benchmarks and best practices.

To perform comprehensive data collection, you or your partner will need to work with your client's records management and information technology teams to identify those areas that are of critical interest to your legal team. You or your partner should have a technically skilled and articulate data collection team that can collaborate with your client to collect data in a professional manner. Your partner should be able to acquire data in "stealth mode" in the middle of the night, or during regular business hours, depending on the needs of your matter. Collection and preservation methods chosen should take into account personnel resources, capital cost and the necessity of keeping business processes running at optimal levels.

The Evolution of Data Collection

In the first chapter of this book, we introduced the concept of the Evidence Management Lifecycle. While not every corporation is there yet, EML becomes a real time-saver and efficiency booster when it comes to data collection for legal matters.

In an EML framework, documents are preserved as they are created by a document management system. They are retained and destroyed according to a records retention policy. When a legal hold is placed, there is no need to trust solely on the cooperation of employees.

The automation enabled by the document management system, and the underlying applications that interface with the EML process, enable faster assessment of where potentially relevant evidence resides and preventing its destruction. To ensure files are not altered or destroyed once a preservation obligation arises, they can either be preserved in place (such as issuing a legal hold within a records management system) or copied to some form of "preservation repository" in a legally defensible manner.

EML allows quick implementation of preservation orders without being overly burdensome to employees or IT. It relieves the corporation of over-preservation tactics such as automated email archiving and dedicated file shares to save everything "just in case." It also simplifies any subsequent search and review of relevant documents. With evidence preservation easily applied within an EML framework, there is a legally defensible business process is in place that lowers the cost and risks associated with preservation, while accelerating electronic discovery when required.

Understanding Data Types and Collection Costs

While you were negotiating the scope of discovery, you may have already limited the potentially responsive data universe to a certain type of data. The following table outlines the three main types of data and their characteristics.

Data Type	Cost of Collection	Characteristics
Active	Easiest to get, least costly.	Documents that "actively" reside on the custodian's computer hard drive or other storage device. Active documents are all those that you can see in a file manager or explorer type of tool. Examples include e-mail and standard office documents like word processing and spreadsheets. Active files are generally easy to access and collect. Challenges include dealing with large volumes of data and preserving file date information. Most requests for production ask for active files.
Archival	Requires restoration, costs vary depending on volume and backup format.	Documents and files stored, often in a compressed format, on off-line devices including backup tapes or disks, floppies, and optical media. Archived documents are harder and more expensive to retrieve than active documents because they often require restoration, have

Data Type	Cost of Collection	Characteristics
		complex file structures, or are on media that can't be accessed at high speeds. Challenges include dealing with old backup formats or tapes that are not cataloged. De-duplication is an additional challenge when faced with multiple backups of the same set of data over time.
Forensic	Most expensive, requires special tools	Documents and files that are hidden or have been erased, fragmented, or damaged, and that can reside on either on-line or off-line storage devices. Forensic collection provides the most detail and is the only approach for retrieving deleted or fragmented files; however it requires an expert to operate special tools and is time consuming. Collect forensically when you need maximum preservation protection such as when you are responding to a specific event like a wrongful termination litigation. Often, the only way to collect data from a PDA is forensically. Due to cost and/or exposure, opposing counsel is usually not willing to provide forensically collected data; therefore, most often the requesting party bears the cost of forensic collection.

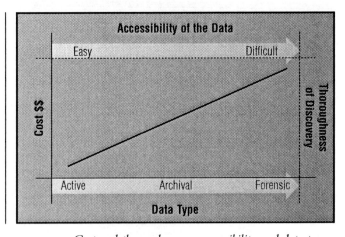

Cost and thoroughness vs. accessibility and data types.

Is it Always Necessary to Collect Forensically?

There are many factors to consider before collecting forensically. The following chart can assist your decision making.

Electronic Discovery vs. Computer Forensics[36]

Factors	Electronic Discovery	Computer Forensics
Number of reviewers	Hundreds at a time	One at a time
Location of reviewers	Geographically dispersed	One place
Type of data	Live (unless other data provided by forensics partner)	Live, resurrected, reconstructed fragments
Recover deleted files	No (unless provided by forensics process)	Yes
Recover Web-based e-mail, chat	No (unless provided by forensics process)	Yes
Encrypted and password protected files	Yes	Yes
Testimony	Fact (protocol)	Opinion (expert)
Who searches and refines searches	Legal team and/or vendor	Forensic technician
Search time	Minutes	Days
Type of collection	Bit image and/or copy	Bit image only
Downtime of client computers	No	Usually
Chain of custody forms	Yes	Yes
Special tools for collection	Yes	Yes
Testifying expert necessary	No	Yes
Cooperation of IT staff	Yes	No
File listings and structures	Yes	Yes
Metadata	Yes	Yes
Production	Native file, print, Web review litigation support load files with images and searchable text	Native file, print

Electronic Discovery vs. Computer Forensics.

---

[36]"Electronic Discovery and Computer Forensics: The Differences You Need to Know," Legal Tech Newsletter, Volume 21, Number 5 (August 2003)

Collect the Data

Because distributed data is the norm in today's business environment, you will find that corporate electronic information is likely located in different geographic locations and systems, controlled by many people and departments. For large organizations, the process of data acquisition from multiple office locations and scores of employees can be difficult without the right tools and processes. You'll want to be sure that your team is experienced at rapidly identifying and properly collecting large quantities of data from multiple sources.

Maintaining data integrity is critical. If you can't authenticate the data, legal risks are created. You'll need to be certain that a complete chain of custody for collected data is maintained to ensure accurate and authenticated information. The appendices of this guide provide useful data collection forms to help you document the chain of custody. Also, be sure that you employ procedures to minimize the risk of damaging, destroying or otherwise compromising evidence during the collection process.

The following activities are crucial for complete and methodical data collection:

- Identify stores of data that may fall within the discovery requirements.

- Maintain chain of custody for any data that is collected.

- Document the source, as well as the rationale, for what data you decide to include in your data set.

- Request a list of all relevant data custodians from your client.

- Match actual name (last, first) with ID (employee numbers, usernames, etc.) used by the data or document management systems. You should also review and cross reference names from prior collections.

- Determine the location of data, from sources such as:
    — Email servers
    — File and print servers
    — Desktops and onsite laptops
    — Field laptops

> — Home computers
>
> — Personal Digital Assistants (PDAs)
>
> — Enterprise Document Management or Records Management repositories
>
> — Shared directories
>
> — Backup tapes
>
> — Disks
>
> — CD-ROMs
>
> — DVD-ROMs
>
> — Cell phones
>
> — Flash memory cards such as "thumb drives"
>
> — MP3 players (modern players support storing data)
>
> — iPods
>
> — Voice over IP phone systems
>
> — Instant Messaging
>
> — Online transactions and databases

- Work with an infrastructure specialist to set up collection servers at optimum network points.

- Use appropriate tools and chain of custody documentation and, when feasible, copy the data over the network to high speed removable hard drives. Be aware that doing a straight copy can result in altered metadata, hence you'll want the assistance of an expert in data collection for electronic discovery. Regardless of whether your electronic discovery partner or your team accomplishes the collection, your partner will need some assistance to access the appropriate areas of the network and specific drives for security reasons.

- If your team performs data copying tasks, you'll need to securely package the data and send or hand-carry it to your electronic discovery partner with chain of custody forms. To maintain chain of custody documentation, your electronic discovery partner must properly receive the data.

- When collecting voice data, make sure you work with the telecommunications specialists. They will know how to pull by date, speaker and/or phone number if their software allows it. Financial firms must retain these recordings. Other firms employ "audio quality" programs to monitor call center agent performance. There may be exculpatory evidence in these systems. Many proprietary systems have a conversion to WAV feature. WAV files can be reviewed and produced on any electronic review system that allows the download of a native file.

The integrity and quality of your electronic data is clearly of paramount importance. To assist you in proper tracking and documentation during this phase of the electronic discovery process, we have included a variety of useful data collection forms in the appendices of this guide.

TIP: Data Collection Efficiency

It is best to do as much live data collection as possible up front rather than having it come in small increments. To optimize the data management and culling, it is best to process and review sets of media (such as quarterly backups), rather than one-at-a-time items (such as daily backups). Once your data is collected, your electronic discovery partner should be able to rapidly produce documents in rolling deliveries.

With that said, however, there is often an unavoidable incremental nature to data collection. You may have to refresh the data set when new information becomes available. Try to keep these collection events as consolidated as possible to make the process easier and more productive for your team.

Your electronic discovery partner should assist you in tracking collection events.

Can You Collect the Data Yourself?

Perhaps in simple cases, with good collaboration of IT staff on both sides, you can perform the data collection yourself. Yet most of the time, you'll be faced with these challenges regarding evidence collection:

• Too much data to review

• Too costly to collect for legal purposes (burden on IT staff)

• Not enough staff to perform actual collection

• Risk of your lawyers or IT personnel being called upon to testify as fact witnesses

- Can't collect data fast enough (for project timeline)

- Don't know how to collect or how to collect responsibly and defensibly (avoiding spoliation, maintaining chain of custody)

- Don't know what to collect

- Don't know where the data is physically

- Don't know how to track a collection project (can't answer the questions, "How much have we collected? How much more do we have to collect? When will we be done collecting?")

- Don't know how to manage the security issues for in-house teams accessing sensitive data

- The team may inadvertently make biased or prejudiced collection decisions.

Risks of Data Collection by Employees

A significant area of risk arises if company employees are allowed to determine which data residing on their computers or storage media is potentially relevant. There are multiple problems inherent in employee data selection and collection:

- There may be an inconsistent understanding or interpretation among employees as to what constitutes relevancy. If a corporate management team tells ten of its employees to gather all of their electronic documents related to a specific topic, there will likely be ten different opinions regarding what is relevant. The attorneys responsible for discovery should clearly define and determine what data is considered relevant, rather than leaving that determination up to the original data custodians.[37]

---

[37]United States v. Philip Morris USA Inc., 327 F. Supp.2d 21 (D.D.C. 2004).

- The lack of a cohesive collection strategy may make the data unreliable. If the data collection activity is too narrow or has the potential for being inconsistent, any changes in the scope or in the issues of the case may drive the need for future rounds of data collection.

- Having employees copy their information over to a centralized location creates a significant risk of data alteration resulting from functions that automatically update data within word processing and spreadsheet programs ("AutoSave"), as well as viral exposure.

- Employees who are aware of relevant documents within their data sets may be inclined to avoid potential legal risks created by the documents; hence they may inappropriately self-cull the data. Other employees may have embarrassing material that could cause them to cull excessively or delete documents.

- Employees who are involved in the data collection are immediately made fair targets for being called to testify regarding the completeness and accuracy of their data collection.

Data Magnitude Explained

When facing the prospect of data collection, many litigation teams are not yet familiar with the sheer magnitude of data stored on CD-ROMs, hard drives and other storage media. The terms "megabytes," "gigabytes," and "terabytes" are commonly used, but often it is difficult to gauge what those data volumes mean in terms of page equivalents. The following conversion table provides a data equivalent overview.

Boxes of Paper	Total Pages	Megabytes; Gigabytes; Terabytes
1	2,500	50 Megabytes
10	25,000	500
20	50,000	1 Gigabyte
100	250,000	5
200	500,000	10
300	750,000	15
400	1,000,000	20
500	1,250,000	25
1,000	2,500,000	50
2,000	5,000,000	100
5,000	12,500,000	250
10,000	25,000,000	500
20,000	50,000,000	1 Terabyte
40,000	100,000,000	2
60,000	150,000,000	3

After terabytes...?

- Comes petabytes and exabytes. A petabyte equals 1000 terabytes, while an exabyte equals 1000 petabytes.
- All words ever spoken by human beings amounts to about five exabytes.[38]

Compared to...?

- The complete works of Shakespeare amount to about 5 megabytes.
- One terabyte is equivalent to 50,000 trees made into paper and printed.
- If digitized, the nineteen million books and other print collections in the Library of Congress would contain about ten terabytes of information.

---

[38]"How Much Information?," a study published by SIMS, October 27, 2003. © 2003 Regents of the University of California. Downloadable at *http://www.sims.berkeley.edu/research/projects/how-much-info-2003/*

The assumptions for this exhibit are that the average banker's box holds 2,500 sheets of paper, and one page of information on average equals 20 kilobytes (.02 megabytes). This page-to-data size conversion factor is conservative. For example, collections consisting largely of emails and spreadsheets may have a conversion factor of .01 or even .005, resulting in two to four times as many "pages" or page-equivalents.

The Importance of Chain of Custody

A defensible chain of custody is clearly vital, yet the passage of time can pose some unexpected challenges. Larger legal cases can often last for years, and information technology teams often experience frequent turnover. It is critically important, therefore, to gather the contact information for both the subject of the data collection as well as the person doing the collecting.

You may want to utilize serial numbers and asset tags to tie the data collected to a specific machine, which thus ties it to a person. You'll also want to track what external devices are on a custodian's machine to ensure knowledge regarding the machine's external media capacity. For example, documenting that the CD drive is a CD-Read Only device will reduce the likelihood that the opposition can charge that CD backups were produced from that custodian's computer.

This physical audit trail to the electronic data can be of crucial importance. Appendix B of this guide provides sample data collection checklists that are useful for managing the process with appropriate documentation. The primary purpose for this level of detail is that the data collection staff will not have to rely on memory should they need to be deposed.

Managing chain of custody includes maintaining physical and/or automated records of chronological and logistical information such as:

- What was the source of the data (custodian and location)?

- Where on the hard drive were individual files physically located?

- What metadata is available, and what files does it link to?

- What was the relationship between emails and their attachments?

- When did the data arrive?

- What was the complete chain of custody up to the production phase of the project?

See the Appendices for sample forms.

Common Data Collection Questions

Are electronic discovery and computer forensics the same thing?
No, electronic discovery and forensics are not the same thing, but forensics is an important subset of the electronic discovery process. The first requirement for electronic discovery is to find and record all necessary "live," or easily accessible, files on a company's computer system. Digital information, however, is not always readily accessible. Some files may be deleted, corrupted or otherwise hidden. In addition to collecting currently active files through "live data" collection (common electronic discovery collection), computer forensics allows the collection of deleted, hidden, password-protected and encrypted files and file fragments.

Electronic discovery of "live data" is essential in most cases, but computer forensics is required in only limited circumstances, such as cases relating to criminal matters, key personnel, bad faith, intellectual property and/or wrongful termination. To reduce the risk of exposing your work product to the opposition, be certain that your electronic discovery partner maintains appropriate confidentiality of information and does not unnecessarily share information with the forensics experts who may be deposed and testify about forensic findings.

What is a program or system file, and why can it be culled?
Program files, like those associated with software applications and operating systems, provide the mechanical ability for items such as documents and spreadsheets to be created and for computers to function. They do not contain any material that the end user has created. Discovery does not include those program files (with file extensions such as ".EXE," ".HLP," ".DLL," ".LST," etc.), thus they are not required and can be culled. A deeper inquiry is necessary if your case involves compiled source code.

Your electronic discovery vendor should maintain a library to identify and remove common application program files such as those installed with Microsoft® Office, so that your reviewers will not need to review the standard templates provided with the programs. For example, Microsoft Word comes with many templates and sample files, which on the surface appear to be user-created files due to their file extensions (.DOT or .DOC). A sophisticated electronic discovery partner can cull these templates and samples, thus your review team won't waste time reviewing them.

How much time does it take?

The amount of time it will take depends on whether it is forensic or active collection — also the number of locations, amount of data, number of drives, and type(s) of drives (server, desktop or laptop). Forensics collection takes longer than active collection; servers take more time than laptops; laptops take longer than desktops. Other variables include the speed of the network and whether or not the servers are RAID servers. In summary, the time required can range from a single day to multiple weeks.

What will custodians' experience be during collection?

This also depends on whether it is forensics or active collection. Individual custodians may be asked to give up their machines for a short amount of time (1 hour or less for active, 1–3 hours for forensics). In forensics collection, special forensics software is used and the hard drive of subject is quarantined from change as data is copied bit by bit. The hard drive from the custodian's computer may be removed and then replaced at the end of the collection. Data can also be collected at night or over the network in some situations.

Why shouldn't attorneys collect the data as they interview witnesses?

Attorneys can assist in collection by identifying individuals to collect, their network drives and any folders which should be excluded or included in a collection. Picking and choosing files by opening them will change the access date and in the case of Microsoft Office documents, can change the last modified date. Attorneys who pick and choose files can be called to testify as to the chain of custody of the data they collected.

Understand What You Have — Early On

While corporate IT personnel may possess the technical skills required to collect data, they may not have the resources, tools, or procedures to analyze, manage and distill the data for the legal process.

An electronic discovery partner is helpful at this point, because they can generate basic reports of what has been collected (e.g., number of files, file types, volume of data, etc.). Your collection partner will be creating an evidentiary log documenting all processes and procedures conducted during the collection process.

This information enables you to make informed decisions before processing the data when preparing for legal proceedings and ensures that the process is defensible. Your electronic discovery partner can also help you store the data and/or images(s) on appropriate media in a secure storage facility, ensuring that it is recoverable over time.

After your data has been collected and you've assessed what you have, the third step of the electronic discovery is data processing. The following chapter details the activities and tools involved to process data for review.

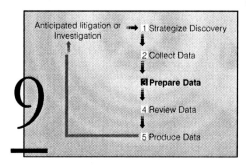

DATA PROCESSING: AGGREGATING FOR THE VISIBILITY

Once data has been collected, you'll need a way to review it in a format that allows full visibility of every responsive aspect. You'll also want the ability to do large-scale data searches of the entire data set, rather than by individual data custodians one at a time.

For this to be done efficiently, those files must be aggregated into a unified database. To create a comprehensive and secure database of original file content and metadata, your electronic data is best managed by converting it into a common viewable format such as HTML or TIFF or Adobe PDF. (Remember, deciding on a review format was an earlier strategy decision point.) The most useful unified databases are fully indexed and optimized for searching and can be output to a variety of formats for review, including the web, databases or paper.

Data processing should include capturing a digital fingerprint (in techno-speak, a unique "hash") of each file for authenticity purposes, documenting the chain of custody, and virus-scanning the files.

To minimize cost and when appropriate, data should be reduced (also known as evidence screening) before full processing. Data reduction includes winnowing out operating system and program files; identifying and reducing duplicates; and culling based on file type, custodian and date ranges. This reduction can include keyword search terms for culling or simply pre-categorization of potentially privileged evidence or non-responsive documents.

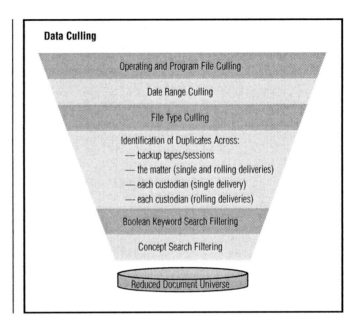

What Is Metadata, and Why Is It Important?

Metadata is often described as "data about the data." It includes information such as file dates, authors, source locations and email routing information that generally does not appear on the printed page. The electronic discovery process is the best method to access such metadata, which can contain important information about who created and reviewed electronic documents and to whom they were distributed.

Metadata is indicative of, but not definitive of, dates, creators of documents and other properties. Metadata is collected and stored differently by each application program. Even versions of the same program can treat metadata differently. Your electronic discovery vendor should help you understand the nuances of metadata and ensure that your data is collected and produced with impeccable chain of custody procedures. You should also make sure that your electronic discovery vendor has the ability to export all types of metadata to your review database.

There are five key types of metadata your electronic discovery partner should identify and manage:

- File system metadata — data that can be obtained or extracted about a file from the file system storing the file.

- Document metadata — data stored in the document about the document. Often this data is not immediately viewable in the application used to create/edit the document but often can be accessed via a "Properties" view.

- Email metadata — data stored in the email about the email. Often this data is not even viewable in email client applications used to create the email. The amount of email metadata available for a particular email varies greatly depending on the email system.

- Vendor-added metadata — data created and maintained by your electronic discovery vendor as a result of processing the item. While some of the vendor-added metadata has direct value to you, much of it is used for process reporting, chain of custody and data accountability.

- Customer-added metadata — data or "work product" created by a customer while reviewing the document set.

Metadata	Description	Type
File Class	Generic class of a document. Examples: "Spreadsheet," "Graphics," "Word Processing"	File System
File Type	File type (or "signature") determined by vendor by analyzing the file (regardless of file extension). Examples: "Microsoft® Excel 2000" or "Word Perfect 5.0"	File System
File Size	File size of the document in bytes.	File System
Date Last Modified	Date and time the file was last saved.	File System
Read Only	Specifies whether a file or folder is read-only, which means that it cannot be changed or accidentally deleted.	File System
Encrypted	Specifies whether a file or folder is encrypted. This is metadata from the file system; not available for e-mails.	File System

Metadata	Description	Type
Title	Title of the document as entered by the author, or already present in the document template.	Document
Subject	Subject of the document as entered by the author, or already present in the document template.	Document
Author	Author of the document, typically automatically entered by the application by reading the local computer's settings. The actual author of the document can typically overwrite this value.	Document
Manager	Manager of the author of the document as entered by the author, or already present in the document template.	Document
Company	Company of the author of the document as entered by the author, or already present in the document template.	Document
To:	Names of the recipients of an e-mail	E-mail
From:	Name of the sender of the e-mail	E-mail
Date:	Sent, received and modified dates for e-mails	E-mail
BCC	Names of blind carbon-copied recipients of an e-mail.	E-mail
Importance	Importance value assigned to e-mail. Examples: "High," "Normal," and "Low"	E-mail
Sender Name	Name of the e-mail sender. This may be a fully qualified e-mail address (ralph.jones@acme.com) or an alias used by the e-mail system (Ralph Jones).	E-mail
Sensitivity	Sensitivity value assigned to e-mail. Examples: "Normal" and "Confidential"	E-mail
Sent On	Date and time the e-mail was sent.	E-mail
Sent On Behalf Of Name	Name of the true sender of the e-mail (whether by proxy or by name that appears in Sender Name).	E-mail
Bates	The Bates range assigned to a document. Because some vendors support producing a document multiple times to multiple parties, a document may have any number of Bates ranges.	Vendor-added
Date Published	Date and time a document, media, shipment or case was published to the data review tool.	Vendor-added

Metadata	Description	Type
Duplicate Status	A flag used to indicate a document is a duplicate of another document in the data collection Extremely useful in filtering out duplicates.	Vendor-added
Read/ Unread	A flag used to track whether an individual user of the data review tool has read a document.	Vendor-added
Categories	List of the categories associated with a document or e-mail.	Customer-added
Annotation Comment	Free-form text of the annotation added by a customer. A single document can have multiple annotations.	Customer-added
Annotation Selected Text	The section of a document about which the annotation was made.	Customer-added

Sophisticated Identification of Duplicates

Just "getting rid of duplicate files" should never be considered as an effective solution. You need to make sure there is a legally defensible audit trail for any duplicate files before you delete them. The question of "who had access to what, and when" is often very relevant and can be missed if duplicate data files are automatically deleted. Experienced litigation support managers recognize the value of identifying duplicates across the whole data set so that the "dupes" can be coded and categorized consistently, which will reduce the time and effort expended by your data review team.

Pitfalls with Email Culling

An overly aggressive, unconditional de-duplication strategy with document sets containing email can lead to undesirable results and significant legal liabilities. Some electronic discovery vendors new to the field practice such a strategy because it results in short-term cost reduction. Yes, there will be fewer documents to review — only one copy of any given item within the entire document set. However, this kind of de-duplication doesn't allow you to see the data in, or produce it from, the other locations or contexts in which that data originally resided. The broader context of a document — who had access to it, and to which emails it was attached — is often critical to the issues of a matter. (see Tips on email chains and threads, and why they matter).

A more sophisticated approach is to flag each instance of a document where it exists in a unique context (electronic discovery professionals often describe the different contexts in terms of different document "chains.")

For example, consider the case in which (1) a word-processed memo is created by Ms. A. She saves it to her computer's hard drive in her "memos" folder. (2) Ms. A then sends an email to her boss explaining the legal risks of the attached memo. (3) Later, Ms. A sends another email to a number of people on the management team of her company, again attaching the same memo, but this time without any legal risk caveats.

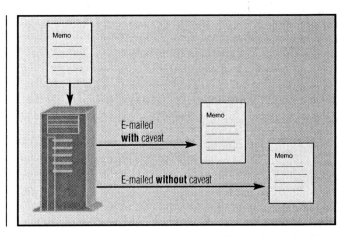

Pitfalls with email culling.

The more junior, less experienced electronic discovery partner might decide that all three instances of the memo are "equal" duplicates and thus provide only the first (or third) instance to the discovery team to review. The critical second instance, demonstrating awareness of legal risks, is then missed. The liability of this approach is compounded should the discovery team later "re-duplicate" the document set at production time.

The fundamental flaw is failing to consider the various contexts in which the memo existed. The sophisticated electronic discovery partner will recognize the three instances of the memo itself as duplicates, but will flag them such that the discovery team reviews each instance within the three very different contexts — only one of which demonstrates the author's (highly relevant) knowledge of the legal risk of the memo.

TIP: The Difference Between Chains and Threads

> *An email "chain" is the email plus its attachments, including files, other emails with their attachments (nest attachments), and embedded links to other documents or web pages.*
>
> *An email "thread" is the history and the progression of an email topic, including the various replies, forwards and added recipients.*

Duplicate Identification Methods

There are three primary methods for identification of duplicates: Backup, Across Case and Within Custodian de-duplication. The preference is your decision. The differences between the three methods are as follows:

Backup de-duplication will look for and retain single copies of documents in the exact same context. If an identical document name, date and file size is found on 10 backup tapes, it can be assumed that it is the same file, and only one copy of the file needs to be preserved. Unless there is bad faith alleged, it is unlikely that you will need to report on each file of the backup tape.

Across Case de-duplication will look for and retain single copies of documents per case. So if an identical document resides with Mr. A, Mr. B and Mr. C, only the first occurrence of the file (i.e., Mr. A's) will be saved.

Within Custodian de-duplication will only de-duplicate a document if multiple copies of that document reside within the same custodian's data set. So if Mr. A and Mr. B each have a copy of a specific document, and Mr. C has two copies, the system will maintain one copy each for Mr. A, Mr. B and Mr. C.

When it comes time to produce, some partners provide another very useful method for de-duplicating: production.

Production de-duplication. Like custodian de-duplication, production de-duplication will only de-duplicate a document if multiple copies of that document reside within the same production set. So, if two identical documents are both marked responsive, non-privileged, the system will only produce one of those documents.

Another pitfall of poorly considered de-duplication is that you may end up producing incomplete email chains, in which the attachments have been lost. For example, you want to avoid the situation where the same file is attached to two different emails, both marked responsive, yet one of the attachments is not produced because it is automatically screened out as "duplicate." This would result in a broken or incomplete chain. Ask your partner if they support a rule that ensures that a chain of emails and attachments are always produced together, and that this rule trumps any de-duplication rules.

Some electronic discovery partners or software packages can only thoroughly de-duplicate emails but not stand-alone files such as word processing documents or spreadsheets. Others are able to do precise file comparisons to identify unique or identical files. You'll want to be sure that your electronic discovery partner can do precise file comparisons for all types of files, not just email.

TIP: The Importance of Email Chains

> *To get full visibility into your data, you'll need access to complete email chains, including the original email and all of its attachments. This is critically important because you often need to produce the entire chain and therefore need to review a chain in its entirety to determine if any single item is confidential or privileged.*

Thorough Data Processing

Data processing for electronic discovery requires expertise in various technologies. Electronic document populations generally contain large volumes of disparate file types. For an electronic discovery project to be successful, this data must be processed and aggregated quickly and reliably.

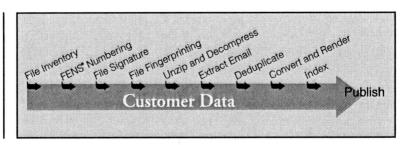

Data Processing.

Data processing steps

- Fully inventory and uniquely number each file in the data population for 100 percent file accountability. Normally, this involves digital fingerprinting (or "hashing") each file for authenticity and chain of custody.

- Be sure that you have a log of all passwords required to access files. Otherwise, it's difficult to secure prompt access to important file information. Make sure that your partner can break the passwords for critical data custodians.

- Uncompress compressed files while maintaining the folder structure of the compressed files. Also, decompression must be done recursively so that if you have a parent ZIP file that contains a set of children ZIP files, all files will be uncompressed and ready for review, rather than just the parent ZIP file.

- Digitally identify each file's signature to determine its true file type rather than relying on the file's extension, which is often inaccurate.

- Remove operating system and program (software application) files.

- Cull your data based on file type, custodian, date ranges, and/or predetermined search terms.

- Flag duplicate files so they may be filtered out during review. You should be able to produce all original native files, including duplicates you may have filtered.

- Extract file content and metadata from the files (e.g., email routing data, file property data and other "hidden" data that can be relevant during discovery).

- Convert all of the electronic documents to common viewable format. Ideally, convert to a higher fidelity, more interactive format like HTML rather than a static format such as TIFF or PDF. This often is most cost effective and enables reviewers to hit-highlight, copy text to the clipboard, and select text or mark annotations. Since HTML is not a paginated format like TIFF or PDF, it provides a far more efficient way to review complex documents like spreadsheets.

At this stage, you have the option of merging your electronic documents with paper documents that have been scanned, and/or optically character recognized (OCRed).

TIP: Bates Numbering Capabilities

In anticipation of discovery, you'll want to have a clear understanding of your electronic discovery partner's capabilities and limitations with respect to Bates numbering. Be sure that you are able to assign multiple Bates numbers to an electronic document in case you'll need to produce it in multiple matters or to multiple recipients. This enables the reuse of information that has already been reviewed for privilege and relevancy, and this will save you time in the review stage. You'll also want to know the legal matter for which it was reviewed and the production sets in which it was included.

Preparing Email

Most often email messages and attachments are stored in the form of self-contained mailbox files that typically reside on network servers, though they may also reside on the data custodian's desktop computer (either manually saved to a hard drive by the user or automatically moved from the active inbox to the hard drive for archiving purposes via rules and email handling settings.) Difficulties can arise if mailbox files are collected and reviewed incorrectly. For example, if an attorney reviews these files from within an email software program, critical content and metadata may change automatically as each file is opened and read, or if it is forwarded or copied. Further, if the mailbox contained unsent messages in the "Outbox," an attorney opening the mailbox may inadvertently send the outbound messages automatically. Upon exit, an automatic "empty recycle bin" rule may be invoked.

Efficiency in review is also difficult due to the sheer volume of email communications in today's workplace. About 31 billion emails are sent daily, a figure which is expected to double by 2006 In addition, usage of instant messaging (IM) is increasing. Nearly 40 percent of U.S. Internet users at home log into one of the IM networks at least once in May 2002, while 31 percent of U.S. business Internet users used IM.[39]

---

[39] These and other metrics for electronic data volumes can be found in "How Much Information?", a report by SIMS Berkeley *http://www.sims.berkeley.edu/research/projects/how-much-info-2003/printable_report.pdf.* Release date: October 27, 2003. © 2003 Regents of the University of California

These percentages can only be expected to rise. Moreover, the increasing use of Voice over IP (using the Internet for telephone communication), stored on servers along with conventional email, adds another source of electronic data to consider.

If your client has a significant amount of electronic communication, you have to open each custodian's email message box at a time. If you're opening messages from within the email software application, you can't do global searches on the attachments associated with the messages. Although you can search the email message content, the attachments provide valuable information that you'll need to access for full data review.

Limitations of Litigation Support Packages

Early litigation support software packages were primarily designed to accommodate scans of paper documents. They have subsequently been upgraded to support TIFF images of electronic documents. Some litigation support packages indicate that they manage electronic documents via tagging and searching the information, but you may not be getting what you need.

To avoid this logistical hassle, you should consider using technology that will allow you to convert native files into TIFF files so you can Bates-stamp the images and automatically track them.

Some electronic litigation support packages can process email but can't create TIFF images of the review set. After legal teams complete the review, they may not be able to accurately or efficiently output the results and reliably track production.

TIP: Taking Out the Garbage

You may find that your client provides a massive amount of data, yet much of it serves no purpose (such as system and software application files that do not contain relevant content). You can save significant amounts of time by having your client's files cataloged so a fast cull can be done to filter those unneeded files. Well-structured, efficient preculling and categorization of data via search terms are highly recommended methods prior to creating the data review/control set.

Time Zone Challenges

When preparing data, your electronic discovery vendor must be able to manage date and time complexities. You may need to combine emails from various offices throughout the nation or the world. This introduces time zone issues (even as common as East Coast vs. West Coast, or daylight vs. standard time). Date/time sequences can be crucial in identifying who knew what when, yet the sequences will be incorrect unless you base it all on a standard such as Greenwich Mean Time (GMT). As an added complexity, Windows® 95 stores dates differently than Windows 2000. Fortunately, all of these date and time issues can be handled by experienced electronic discovery vendors.

Once your data is properly converted into a unified database and published to a common repository, you are ready to begin the fourth and often most time consuming step of a discovery project, the document review step.

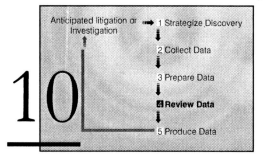

DATA REVIEW: FAST AND THOROUGH METHODS

During the discovery phase of large or complex cases, there can be significant time and resource burdens associated with document review. Reviewing printed versions of electronic materials can be a time-consuming process. It is also subject to risks of omission due to "reviewer's fatigue," resulting in potential misidentification and misclassification of relevant and privileged evidence.

To reduce fatigue and meet tight electronic discovery response deadlines imposed by courts and government agencies, legal teams should use reliable electronic data review tools that are fast and efficient. Pick the vendor or products that enable this. Review tools must scale to meet the demands of a project of any size and provide means for tracking progress and ensuring that all materials are reviewed thoroughly and accurately.

Have in place a protocol that maps technology and techniques to the review goals. You may want to create "if yes/if no" decision trees, along with category or issue coding lists to help guide review. Avoid the natural tendency to treat electronic documents just like paper documents. For example, a traditional approach to a paper review is to code documents by type such as "memos/letters, spreadsheets, notices, presentations, meeting agendas/minutes, etc." Most electronic discovery partners will identify document types automatically via a reliable, repeatable signature process, which is not subject to the natural variances with coding done by humans. Admittedly, these automated processes do not differentiate meeting minutes from memos (instead, they will identify both as word processed documents). Yet at the end of the day, the task is to make a quick, sound judgment as to the document's relevancy and/or confidentiality/privilege status. Any further coding is often a waste of time given the benefits of accurate full text searching.

TIP: What You Don't See on Paper

When electronic information is directly converted to paper for review, much information can be lost and therefore never seen. Things such as metadata, linkages between email messages and attachments, hidden or changed text in word processing documents, formulas and hidden rows and columns in spreadsheets are not printed to paper. Therefore, you'll want to utilize the appropriate electronic discovery tools and processes.

This chapter covers some general review tips and important considerations when evaluating review tools and technologies.

Safeguard the Data

Once the data has been gathered and aggregated, it needs to be safeguarded so you can confidently review it with security. Make sure your review system is redundant and protected. Make sure your electronic discovery partner utilizes the latest in data center security technologies and the best practices in deploying, handling and protecting assets and your information.

The data center should be physically secured, of course (accessible only by keycard system, for example), but also electronically secure. Protections should include utilizing state-of-the-art double firewall systems to fully isolate the hosted data and encrypt SSL connections. Other standard protections include a robust intrusion detection system. Email correspondence with your electronic discovery partner can be conducted using 512-bit encryption and digital certificates. Post-litigation protections should include wipes of the project data and return of your materials.

Ways to Reduce Search and Review Time

There is a misperception about electronic discovery that you'll have to read thousands of documents online. In reality, the sophisticated search capabilities available in today's electronic discovery data review tools reduce the document count dramatically. For example, you decide whether you want to review the final documents on screen or on paper.

For the most accurate and efficient data review process, you should consider utilizing a web-based (online) review tool that enables your legal team to search, organize, categorize, annotate, cull and produce information. The goal is to reduce the time and resources you need to allocate to the search and review process while protecting the integrity of your client's data. Online discovery enables remote, secure access to your data for concurrent review by members of your team.

Sophisticated online review tools also enable instant messaging capability. This helps save time by bridging the geographic gap between reviewers. Your team can immediately clarify document review criteria or other questions by sending a secure instant message to a peer or to all reviewers on the team.

Combine Electronic and Hard Copy

You'll want the ability to import hard copy images and associated text into your data review set, so you can review them concurrently with electronic documents. Make sure your vendor can create and control a master data repository containing both paper-based imaged documents and electronic documents. Usually this means you'll want them to convert hard copy to TIFF images, preserving all associated page-level text, Bates numbers, and maintaining the document groupings based upon your specifications.

Email Chains

There is often more to an email than the distribution list, subject line and body. Email messages are complex items with "chains" — i.e., any number of attachments and nested attachments (emails attached to emails attached to emails…). To expedite your review, you want a tool that displays or maps the complete chain and allows you to quickly and directly navigate to any item in the chain. Sophisticated tools also clearly display the chain's custodian and provide basic information about each item such as its file type, ID number, the number of "descendent" items beneath each branch of the chain, and each items' coding or category information.

Concept Searching

Being able to find, review and produce electronic documents that are conceptually related to initial search queries allows legal teams to identify and review relevant documents more quickly and more accurately than traditional search tools. Unlike keyword searching which requires skillful use of Boolean operators like "AND" and "OR," concept searching has no required formatting or syntax — reviewers can enter a natural language query or paste entire paragraphs from a relevant document, and within seconds receive a list of all related documents, ranked by relevancy. Concept searching often helps a review team understand the nature or themes of their document set quickly, can aid in the review prioritization of different segments of the document set, and can help reviewers form better, more comprehensive keyword searches.

Efficiency of the Tool

When evaluating document review technology, view efficiency of the tool as the primary predictor of the speed of your review. The technology's overall efficiency becomes especially important when attempting to extrapolate the total cost of a document review.

Here are a few points to keep in mind when comparing review technologies:

Tools that fit. The most important way to minimize the cost of a discovery project is to use efficient tools that fit your review team's workflow. Compare the ways different applications support common tasks like searching, categorizing, and browsing.

For example, while the time to actually run a search is important, also consider the time it takes to define the search and review the results. Also consider the flexibility of the search user interface: How many criteria can be combined? How easy is it to add and remove search criteria? How easy is it to save a search and pull up a saved search? Can saved searches be shared across the review team?

Individual vs. family. Consider how well the application in question supports efficient review of complex email families or chains. Ask questions like, "Does the application support categorizing or tagging an entire chain at once?"

Mouse clicks and shortcuts. If you really want to compare application efficiency rather than performance (single dimension), start counting mouse clicks and key presses. Less is more. Make sure your review tool can be "driven" by a keyboard as well as a mouse — keyboard input is roughly three times faster than a mouse.[40]

Review for Privilege and Relevance

Create a list of all counsel names and law firm names so that potentially privileged items can be separated from the data set right at the beginning of the review cycle. The greater the number of potentially privileged documents you identify, the greater protection you provide for your client and the faster you can complete the review process.

STEP ONE: Define the Criteria for Relevance and Privilege

While this may seem like an obvious step, establishing the criteria for categorizing documents as potentially relevant or privileged can have a profound impact on the effectiveness of the data review. The larger the number of reviewers on your project, the more important it becomes to clearly document criteria for categorizations. Any ambiguities in the criteria will prolong the review and may delay the project.

STEP TWO: Review for Relevance

- Conduct a first-pass review of the documents for relevance, and flag the questionable documents.

- Conduct a second-pass review of the subset of documents that have been marked as potentially relevant.

STEP THREE: Review for Privilege

- Create a privilege log. Sophisticated review tools automatically track privilege information and allow you to generate a privilege log at the end of your review.

- Search your relevant documents for privilege with firm names, attorney names and other indications of privilege. Your electronic discovery vendor will be able to help you construct a search. Conduct a first-pass

---

[40]Study conducted by F1-Key LLC *(www.f1key.com)*

review of documents for privilege. Flag privileged documents and record the privilege claim. Flag partially privileged documents to be redacted later.

- Conduct a second-pass review of documents for privilege.

- Redact documents that are partially privileged, and maintain a privilege log.

Proper Indexing Is Crucial

A common problem in data review, as well as during data processing, is a lack of completely indexed data. The quality of the indexing is very important, as it is the key to finding the data you need. A variety of indexing methods are possible, the use of which depends on the nature of your data.

For email, it is best to extract all the email metadata (including the body of the email) and attachments and then build an index for searching. In their original form, email messages and their attachments are contained in a single large "mailbox" file. For example, Microsoft® Exchange mail systems typically store emails in a ".PST" file while Lotus Notes® mail systems typically store emails in an ".NSF" file. If you were to do a keyword search on a mailbox file, you would not be able to search the individual email and attachments within that file. Once all the content is extracted from a mailbox, however, each individual email message, all its metadata and any attachments are available for searching. For example, you can then pull up only those documents that were sent or received by a particular person. There are some intriguing desktop search tools emerging in the marketplace, yet none of them have a defensible way to extract the emails that have hits in them. Check in to discoveryresources.org for news on such tools.

For all other files, it is best to do native file indexing, because those files do not have the same limitations that affect email files.

The Right Search Terms

One pitfall in the review stage is the use of overly broad search terms (such as "office," "company name," "contract," etc.), which can result in a massive number of irrelevant hits. You need to ensure that your search parameters and mechanism appropriately narrows the resulting data set. You'll want to be able to do things like proximity searches (such as looking for the word "contract" within a number of words or another word, such as "contract w/5 of employment"). You'll also want your review tool's search engine to do specific sub searches within metadata fields such as "to," "from" and "subject."

Using electronic discovery data review tools, data searches can be done on an impressive number of terms. Advanced tools can do simultaneous searches in excess of 2,500 characters. Depending on word count, that can average between 300 and 500 words during a single search. Make sure that your search tool allows you to exclude certain sets of data from your search. This is critical when your data is flowing into the system at different times.

Data File Extensions — There's More Than Meets the Eye

Unless you're using appropriate search technology, data file extensions can be problematic during the review stage. As an example, the file extension for a Microsoft Word document, which is traditionally ".DOC," can be changed to other file extensions such as ".EXE," ".PSD," ".XLS," etc. It is very simple for a data custodian who does not want information to be easily discovered to alter file extensions within his or her data set. Some programs even change file extensions on their own. For instance, when "auto-saving" documents, some word processing programs save temporary, at times hidden, ".TMP" files.

Consider the scenario where Mr. Smith alters the file extensions on a set of confidential documents. Later, the data reviewer who gathers Mr. Smith's computer files and searches the entire data set for "*.DOC" (which is supposed to turn up all word processing document file types) will not find all document files. The benefit of using sophisticated data review tools is that they will search through all content, thus eliminating the risk of incorrect file extensions.

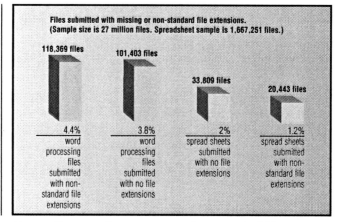

Percent of common document types with non standard file extensions.

Time Crunch

Despite the best intentions, litigation teams don't always allow enough time during the planning process for data review, which can cause a problematic time crunch. If you are in a situation where you need to quickly assign additional document reviewers to your project, you'll want to be sure your vendor doesn't charge you on a per-seat license basis, otherwise your costs will go up. Potentially more detrimental than the extra seat fees could be the delays in purchasing the licenses, setting up the new accounts and/or installing new software.

Some law firms use data review tools that are provided on a per-seat basis and share individual passwords among multiple data reviewers. Aside from potentially violating software license agreements, such activity results in reduced security and data reliability. You should be able to authenticate exactly who had access to confidential client data and who reviewed each document. Every system user should be accessing the data set via his or her unique account and password.

The Dark Side of Unprotected Desk-side Data Review

When a company provides data or access to custodian desktops to its law firm, the attorneys are often tempted to do a desk-side, native file review of the material by opening and identifying which files meet the relevance criteria, and then copying the files over to another location. The following risks of doing an unprotected review of data are significant:

- It increases the risk of infecting files with viruses.

- Opening and/or moving files that have auto-date or auto-path features activated can change dates and file path references associated with the file, even though you didn't intentionally modify the content. This is where modern applications with default "AutoSave" features can get you into big trouble.

- Drag and drop activity with files can also automatically change file reference dates, for example, the Create date. If your legal proceeding is date sensitive, you can inadvertently cause the data to be included or excluded from the "response set."

- Modern email systems are often configured to automatically send email stored in the "outbox" every few minutes. Depending on the state of the mailbox when the custodian last accessed it, this auto-send feature can cause inadvertent transmission of emails by the reviewer.

- Legal teams can encounter unwanted liability if their desktop reviews result in an alteration, damage or total erasure of an important piece of evidence.

After your litigation team has performed a detailed review of your client's data, you'll be ready for the fifth and final step of a discovery project, producing document sets to the requesting parties.

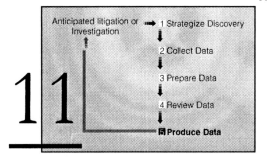

DATA PRODUCTION: SPEED, FLEXIBILITY AND ACCURACY

Once your team has reviewed all documents associated with the discovery process, the relevant non-privileged data set must be delivered to parties such as opposing counsel, partner firms, outside counsel or the requesting government agency. You'll want to be sure that your electronic discovery vendor can provide a variety of delivery options, including Web repositories, exports to other database environments, native files and paper.

Gap-free Bates Production

It is common for files to require some level of manual intervention for successful processing. Files that are encrypted, password-protected and/or those containing macros need special attention to make them print-ready. The challenge during production is that you'll want all of the documents produced in a specific order to maintain an appropriate Bates numbering sequence. Therefore, rather than printing directly from a file, it is best to convert the file into TIFF format and then print it. Any problematic files will be discovered during the TIFF creation stage and can be addressed prior to printing. This prevents confusion, eliminates labor-intensive assembly and assures consistent, gap-free Bates numbering.

Readability and Fonts

Having the appropriate fonts loaded into the production system is vital to properly rendering and producing the wide variety of files generally found in electronic data sets. Documents are often created using a surprising number of standard and nonstandard fonts. If a font is not available, font substitution occurs that can result in visual distortion such as overlays and other alterations. You'll want to be sure that all fonts are available so documents can be produced in the original format used by the data custodian.

TIP: Data Production Complexities

> *Your electronic discovery service provider can help you identify which sorts of files are likely to "fail" during the production step. Complications such as password production, macros or presentations files that are too large are common examples that can cause production limitations. You'll want to make sure that your service provider can handle the file complexities and provide detailed exception reporting for file output and, if necessary, export native files for review and production.*

Multiple Production Options

A crucial aspect of production is accurately and reliably tracking document productions so you know what documents went to which recipients on specific dates. All production information should be tracked within the vendor's database. Your vendor should also provide you with the option of producing the same documents to multiple recipients, with separate tracking numbers for each, and, if desired, with different Bates numbers. Make sure your vendor allows you to search for a document based on a Bates number, so if you are presented with an individual page at deposition time, you can retrieve the entire document to view the page in context and make sure it is what you produced.

TIP: Bates Numbering Capabilities

> *In anticipation of discovery, you'll want to have a clear understanding of your electronic discovery partner's capabilities and limitations with respect to Bates numbering. Be sure that you are able to assign multiple Bates numbers to an electronic document in case you'll need to produce it in multiple matters or to multiple recipients. This enables the reuse of information that has already been reviewed for privilege and relevancy, and this will save you time in the review stage. You'll also want to know the legal matter for which it was reviewed and the production sets in which it was included.*

Problems with Do-it-yourself Production

What you print does not always capture everything in a computer file. Often when producing spreadsheets, the selected print area within a document does not contain all the content of the file. You'll need to be sure that any hidden rows, columns and worksheets are unhidden. Spreadsheets also pose the problem of cell contents that are too large for the column or row, resulting in truncated text or placeholder content for numerical data that appears as "######." To prevent this, you'll need the cells to be resized so all the content is visible. Your electronic discovery vendor should offer the option of performing automatic electronic formatting to reveal such content in spreadsheets. After all the content has been made visible, it is then appropriate to convert the file to HTML, TIFF or PDF.

Producing the Right Documents

You don't want to inadvertently produce privileged or irrelevant documents to the opposition. Mishaps at this stage can be devastating to your case. Be certain that your vendor has strict quality control methods in place for document production. Production project managers should clearly understand the data review plan and the methods for data production. You'll want to be confident that your data production is fast, clean and accurate.

Native File Productions

Certain segments of the government are leading the charge for native file productions.

The downside of simply erasing privileged or non responsive documents from a hard disk yourself is that nothing is really erased. An additional step of wiping the drive of remnants of deleted files would be necessary or you would, in essence, be giving up the material you so carefully erased. Also, keeping track, file by file, of what is responsive or not is difficult without a database overlaying the individual files. Even so, it is easier to work on native an individual and almost impossible as a team.

There are electronic discovery vendors offering "pure" native review. Pure native review is accomplished by:

- Having reviewers access a central server containing the Microsoft Office applications, the Adobe, Graphics viewers, Visio etc to display the documents.
- Having a copy of the above files for each reviewer

- Having a 3rd party viewer on the desktop of each individual.

The file must be loaded into memory. Where the original application is opening the file, reviewers can widen and unhide columns, look for comments and search hits via a find command. When using a 3rd party viewer, reviewers are limited to one view, unless the original native file is available for download.

Most electronic discovery partners, regardless of review method, can provide you with a hard drive containing only the responsive, non-privileged files as part of their normal export process.

Prior to agreeing to a native file production, understand that your opponent will have access to the original file, with the hidden columns, tracked changes, comments and versioning history.

Some government agencies are encouraging the use of electronic vaults where they can search and review material without incurring the cost of processing it.

12

CLOSING THE LOOP

The document productions are complete and discovery is over.

It is now time to make sure that all produced material (native or page) gets loaded back into your evidence repository. Make sure that multiple productions get loaded so that the different Bates numbers and markings are captured. Make sure the dates of production are noted, if not in the evidence system, in another system with the details of the court, date of production, and matter name for easier productions in future litigations. Many a time, good faith is established by producing material that has been reviewed and produced in previous litigation while the new material is being collected and reviewed.

In addition, before jumping into your next challenge, take a little time to ask yourself and your discovery team a few questions. The answers to these questions just might help you save time and money the next time around.

- Did you meet your discovery objectives?

- Was there a favorable outcome to the case?

- Was your electronic discovery plan defensible?

- Were your time expectations met?

- Were your time expectations reasonable?

- Did you have the right team players?

- Was order brought to the chaos of the data needed for review?

- Did the productions go smoothly?

- Did you reduce the cost of review for the enterprise?

- Did you reduce the risk of sanctions or malpractice for outside counsel?

It's 4:45 p.m. and the project team is celebrating the successful settlement of a two-year investigation. War stories abound. Heroes are feted and the goats of the project are pilloried. The lead attorney gets up to leave, talking about an early family dinner and seeing his children before bed time.

His cell phone rings. It's the lead partner on the case. And no, he's not calling with congratulations. A civil suit has been filed, asking for documents from your investigation...

Round tripping

We need to emphasize that, even when using a third party for discovery production, it is imperative that the final discovery work product is round-tripped back to the enterprise and stored, preferably, in a secure document management system, where it will be searchable and accessible in the future. This ensures that the discovery product may serve as a baseline for future litigation events.

Returning evidence and work product to the enterprise's document management system completes the evidence lifecycle. Once you have preserved responsive records and used them in a matter, you want to make them easily available for the future, unlike our hapless lead partner in the case above.

Fortunately, with a complete Evidence Management Lifecycle that links document management with legal holds and electronic discovery, you can save time the next time around. You can retain indefinitely the evidence in its own repository — perhaps back to the enterprise's home ECM system but also very easily to a separate secure repository.

In this way, you keep all records in one logical (though perhaps not physical) place. You eliminate reinventing the evidence collection wheel for any similar, future matters and tighten the integration across the technology-enabled business processes of creating, capturing, preserving and discovering documents.

APPENDIX

Appendix A: Protecting Yourself Prior to a Lawsuit

Safeguarding work product

You must not wipe data from your drives or otherwise tamper with potential electronic evidence once you are under investigation or targeted with a lawsuit. Law firms may want to consider protecting their work product, which is not considered evidence.

People who share documents with others in electronic form may want to consider metadata wiping programs as a proactive way to shield prying eyes from their thought processes. These tools will allow you to rid files of the remnants of your tracked changes, versions, and other historical artifacts. Data wiping is clearly not to be used when you are the target of an investigation or a lawsuit, nor can it be used once litigation has begun or spoliation letters have been sent.

Microsoft itself now offers a complementary metadata wiping program. It does not work on all versions of Office, but if your applications are reasonably up to date, it should work for you.
http://www.microsoft.com/downloads/details.aspx?FamilyID= 144e54ed-d43e-42ca-bc7b-5446d34e5360&displaylang=en

Another favorite of the legal community is Payne Consulting's Metadata Assistant. This will allow you to wipe the versioning, track changes, reset the edit time and wipe the author of a document. It also wipes hyperlinks, which can give opposing counsel a peek into how you organize your firm's data. This is a fantastic product to use, even to look at documents that have been provided to you by the other side to see what metadata data hides within. There is a complementary demo of this product on the following site:

http://www.payneconsulting.com/public/products/ProductDet ail.asp?nProductID=34

Wiping your computer

It is true that everything you type into your computer or view from the web on your computer can find its way to your hard drive permanently. This means your online chat, your yahoo email, your bank account password and the confidential client documents that you are drafting or reviewing can resurface. Before you become the target of legal proceedings, consider setting up a wiping program on your PC to clean out those data closets. This will also minimize the damage to you or your clients should your PC be stolen.

Accessdata **(www.accessdata.com)** has a product called SecureClean to permanently erase your leftover data. They also have a whole-disk wiper, which is useful prior to donating a computer.

BC-Wipe is a shareware version of a wiping program. Use a wiping program prior to donating your computer or returning your leased computer. It is the equivalent of shredding your documents before disposing of them. You can find shareware at sites like **www.tucows.com.**

Protecting your company

A document retention policy that is both implemented and monitored can dramatically reduce your exposure. When implementing a practice, including wiping, it is best to document it with a formal policy. Make sure you have provisions to suspend the policy for a "legal hold."

Appendix B: Top Ten Methods of Learning More

Top 10 ways to educate yourself about electronic discovery
(low or no cost)

1. Look for supersites

Visit *www.discoveryresources.org*, a compendium of white papers,
news and jobs involving electronic discovery
Visit *www.complianceresources.org*, for compliance news and white
papers

2. Go to classes

Glasser Legal Works conferences: *http://www.legalwks.com/*

3. Read the books

Essentials of Electronic discovery: Finding and Using Electronic Data,
Joan Feldman *http://www.forensics.com/html/essentials_ED.html*

Electronic Discovery and Evidence, Michael Arkfeld
http://www.arkfeld.com/elec_summary2.htm

Electronic Discovery Law and Practice, Adam Cohen and David Lender

Electronic Evidence, Alan M. Gahtan

Hacking Exposed: Computer Forensics, Davis, Phillips, Cowen

Litigation Readiness: Mastering the Inevitable, Stevens and Dubey

4. Attend the webcasts

http://www.fiosinc.com/webinar.html
http://www.acca.com/education/ cle.php (Now called ACC, a subset of
their CLEs will assist corporate counsel face the electronic discovery
challenge)
http://www.abanet.org/cle/ (The ABAs CLEs, a subset of their CLEs will
be directed at e-discovery practitioners)

5. Download the demos

www.grc.com (Spyware prevention)
www.payneconsulting.com (Metadata wiper for sharing documents)
www.accessdata.com (Password cracking, disk cleaning)

6. Read the case law

Zubulake I, Zubulake v. UBS
Warburg LLC 217 F.R.D. 309 S.D.N.Y., 2003

Zubulake II, Zubulake v. UBS
Warburg LLC, 2003 WL 21087136 S.D.N.Y., 2003

Zubulake III, Zubulake v. UBS
Warburg LLC 216 F.R.D. 280 S.D.N.Y., 2003

Zubulake IV, Zubulake v. UBS
Warburg LLC, 220 FRD 212 S.D.N.Y., 2003

Zubulake V, Zubulake v. UBS
Warburg LLC 2004 WL 1620866 S.D.N.Y., 2004

Residential Funding Corp. v. DeGeorge Fin. Corp., 306 F.3d 99
(2d Cir. 2002)

Arthur Andersen LLP v. U.S., 125 S.Ct. 2129 (2005)

Coleman (Parent) Holdings, Inc. v. Morgan Stanley & Co., Inc.,
2005 WL 67071 (Fla. Cir. Ct. Mar. 1, 2005)

7. Look into organizations creating the context for electronic discovery

http://www.thesedonaconference.org/
(practitioners and vendors create standards)

http://www.fjc.gov/public/pdf.nsf/lookup/ElecDi12.pdf/$file/ElecDi12.pdf
(ABA committee recommends additions to the federal rules)

www.arma.org
(records management generally)

http://www.sochaconsulting.com/referencemodel.htm
(towards cost predictability and data exchange standards)

8. Keep up with the industry

Dennis Kennedy, *www.denniskennedy.com*
(legal technology in general)

Ken Withers, *www.kenwithers.com*
(educating the federal judiciary on electronic discovery, state
and the new Federal Rules)

Ediscoverylaw.com, Preston Gates' wonderful database/blog of caselaw

Soundevidence.discoveryresources.org-blog for e-discovery community

Ben Edelman, *www.benedelman.org*
(Harvard law student expert witness on Internet and spyware issues)

9. Check out vendor sites:

www.ndci.com (pictures of backup media)
www.fticonsulting.com (Ringtail, case management)
www.onlinesecurity.com (incident response)
www.newtechnology.com (grandfather of forensics)
www.guidancesoftware.com (Windows/network based acquisition)
www.fiosinc.com (discovery management and electronic discovery simplified)
www.krollontrack.com (electronic discovery)
www.legaltechnologygroup.com (technical attorney practice)
www.applieddiscovery.com (now part of Lexis, electronic discovery)
www.dolphinsearch.com (conceptual searching)
www.attenex.com (conceptual visualization)

10. Go to conferences and gather the materials from the exhibitors

www.legaltech.com (New York is the largest show)
www.abatechsow.com (one of the oldest conferences)
www.americanconference.com (industry specific e-discovery conferences)

Appendix C: Switching Vendors in Midcase

Sometimes, by design or necessity, you must move a client's data from vendor to vendor during an electronic discovery project. At risk are chain of custody and authenticity of data.

Optimally, this eventuality will be considered and planned for during the contracting part of the project.

When it becomes clear that you must move the data, talk with of the designated contacts separately to address any issues, substantive or emotional, which may arise. Consider a joint teleconference to introduce the designated contacts and to set the context of this short term alliance to accomplish the transfer without impacting timelines or authenticity of the data. Provide both of your vendors with written lists of what you are expecting.

For example, you will need, for yourself and your new vendor:

• A copy of the chain of custody for the media you sent them

• A listing of any manipulation done to the data on the media, if anything other than the original data is to be used by the new vendor

• An inventory of what is being shipped

• A shipping number and carrier for the data

• A contact name and number for issue resolution

The new vendor should immediately unpack and verify the contents of the shipment, making formal note to you of any discrepancies. The contents of the media should be verified. It is not uncommon for media to be unreadable. Metadata should be checked, particularly date metadata, to make sure the data was transferred using evidence quality copy measures. These are problems to be resolved in the first week of a data transfer.

You may consider requesting that the first vendor retain copies of your materials for a period of time to ensure a safe handoff.

While no vendor wants to see their data shipped to another vendor, it does happen. Professional vendors will make the experience as stress free as possible for their client.

Appendix D: Electronic Discovery Templates

In using the following template, please keep in mind that "less is more". Pick and choose from what is presented here to match the specifics of your case and jurisdiction. These are "kitchen sink" requests, which are appropriate for the most extreme types of electronic discovery where spoliation is likely and in criminal matters. You will want to pare these down for normal commercial matters or deploy them as is and negotiate them down during your pretrial conferences.

Asking for more than you need can cause a judge to disallow your requests or award costs. It also opens you up to being asked for the same type and form of information.

Soft copy of these templates are available at **www.fiosinc.com.**

Form spoliation letter to opposing counsel

[date]

[address]

re: [matter (, case number)]

Dear: _____,

By this letter, you and your client{s} are hereby given notice not to destroy, conceal or alter any paper or electronic files and other data generated by and/or stored on your client's {clients'} computers and storage media (e.g., hard disks, floppy disks, backup tapes), or any other electronic data, such as voice recordings. As you know, your client's {clients'} failure to comply with this notice can result in severe sanctions being imposed by the Court {and liability in tort} for spoliation of evidence or potential evidence.

Through discovery we expect to obtain from you a number of documents and things, including files stored on your client's {clients'} computers and your client's {clients'} computer storage media. {As part of our initial discovery efforts, you [are hereby served with/will soon receive] [initial/supplemental] interrogatories and requests for documents and things.}

In order to avoid spoliation, you will need to provide the data requested on original media. Do not reuse any media to provide this data.

{Although [we may bring/have brought] a motion for an order preserving documents and things from destruction or alteration, your client's {clients'} obligation to preserve documents and things for discovery in this case arises in law and equity independently from any order on such motion.}

Electronic documents and the storage media on which they reside contain relevant, discoverable information beyond that which may be found in printed documents. Therefore, even where a paper copy exists, we [seek/will seek] all documents in their electronic form along with information about those documents contained on the media. We also [seek/will seek] paper printouts of only those documents that contain unique information after they were printed out (such as paper documents containing handwriting, signatures, marginalia, drawings, annotations, highlighting and redactions) along with any paper documents for which no corresponding electronic files exist.

Our discovery requests [ask/will ask] for certain data on the hard disks, floppy disks and backup media used in your client's {clients'} computers, some of which data are not readily available to an ordinary computer user, such as "deleted" files and "file fragments." As you may know, although a user may "erase" or "delete" a file, all that is really erased is a reference to that file in a table on the hard disk; unless overwritten with new data, a "deleted" file can be as intact on the disk as any "active" file you would see in a directory listing.

Accordingly, electronic data and storage media that may be subject to our discovery requests and that your client{s} are obligated to maintain and not alter or destroy, include but are not limited to the following:

Introduction: description of files and file types sought

All digital or analog electronic files, including "deleted" files and file fragments, stored in machine-readable format on magnetic, optical or other storage media, including the hard drives or floppy disks used by your client's {clients'} computers and their backup media (e.g., other hard drives, backup tapes, floppies, Jaz cartridges, CD-ROMs) or otherwise, whether such files have been reduced to paper printouts or not. More specifically, your client{s} is {are} to preserve all of your emails, both sent and received, whether internally or externally; all word-processed files, including drafts and revisions; all spreadsheets, including drafts and revisions; all databases; all CAD (computer-aided design) files, including drafts and revisions; all presentation data or slide shows produced by presentation software (such as Microsoft PowerPoint); all graphs, charts and other data produced by project management software (such as Microsoft Project); all data generated by calendaring, task management and personal information management (PIM) software (such as Microsoft Outlook or Lotus Notes); all data created with the use of personal data assistants (PDAs), such as PalmPilot, Blackberry, or other Windows CE-based or Pocket PC devices; all data created with the use of document management software or Customer Relationship Management (CRM) software; all data created with the use of paper and electronic mail logging and routing software; all Internet and Web-browser-generated history files, caches and "cookies" files generated at the workstation of each employee and/or agent in your client's {clients'} employ and on any and all backup storage media; and any and all other files generated by users through the use of computers and/or telecommunications, including but not limited to voice mail.

Further, you are to preserve any log or logs of network use by employees or otherwise, whether kept in paper or electronic form, and to preserve all copies of your backup tapes and the software necessary to reconstruct the data on those tapes. We may request complete, bit-by-bit "mirror" evidentiary image copy of the storage media of each and every personal computer (and/or workstation) and network server in your control and custody containing material potentially responsive in this matter, as well as image copies of all hard drives retained by you and no longer in service, but in use at any time from _____ to the present.

Your client{s} is {are} also not to pack, compress, purge or otherwise dispose of files and parts of files unless a true and correct copy of such files is made.

Your client{s} is {are} also to preserve and not destroy all passwords, decryption procedures (including, if necessary, the software to decrypt the files); network access codes, ID names, manuals, tutorials, written instructions, decompression or reconstruction software, and any and all other information and things necessary to access, view and (if necessary) reconstruct the electronic data we [are requesting/will request] through discovery.

1. **Business Records:** [All documents and information about documents containing backup and/or archive policy and/or procedure, document retention policy, names of backup and/or archive software, names and addresses of any offsite storage provider, records management and enterprise content management systems]. [between the following dates]. [at the following locations]. [in the following departments]. [about the following issues].

   a. All email and information about email (including message contents, header information and logs of email system usage) {sent or received} by the following persons:

   [list names, job titles]

   b. All other email and information about email (including message contents, header information and logs of email system usage) containing information about or related to:

   [insert detail]

   c. All databases (including all records and fields and structural information in such databases), containing any reference to and/or information about or related to:

   [insert detail]

   d. All logs of activity (both in paper and electronic formats) on computer systems and networks that have or may have been used to process or store electronic data containing information about or related to:

[insert detail]

e. All word processing files, including prior drafts, "deleted" files and file fragments, containing information about or related to:

[insert detail]

f. With regard to electronic data created by application programs which process financial, accounting and billing information, all electronic data files, including prior drafts, "deleted" files and file fragments, containing information about or related to:

[insert detail]

g. All files, including prior drafts, "deleted" files and file fragments, containing information from electronic calendars and scheduling programs regarding or related to:

[insert detail]

h. All electronic data files, including prior drafts, "deleted" files and file fragments about or related to:

[insert detail]

2. **Online Data Storage on Network Attached Storage, Mainframes and Minicomputers:** With regard to online storage and/or direct access storage devices attached to your client's {clients'} mainframe computers and/or minicomputers: they are not to modify or delete any electronic data files, "deleted" files and file fragments existing at the time of this letter's delivery, which meet the definitions set forth in this letter, unless a true and correct copy of each such electronic data file has been made and steps have been taken to assure that such a copy will be preserved and accessible for purposes of this litigation.

3. **Offline Data Storage, Backups and Archives, Floppy Diskettes, Tapes and Other Removable Electronic Media:** With regard to all electronic media used for offline storage, including magnetic tapes and cartridges and other media that, at the time of this letter's delivery, contained any electronic data meeting the criteria listed in paragraph 1 above: Your client {clients} is {are} to stop any

activity that may result in the loss of such electronic data, including rotation, destruction, overwriting and/or erasure of such media in whole or in part. This request is intended to cover all removable electronic media used for data storage in connection with their computer systems, including magnetic tapes and cartridges, magneto-optical disks, floppy diskettes and all other media, whether used with servers, personal computers, minicomputers or mainframes or other computers, and whether containing backup and/or archive data sets and other electronic data, for all of their computer systems.

4. **Replacement of Data Storage Devices:** Your client {clients} is {are} not to dispose of any electronic data storage devices and/or media that may be replaced due to failure and/or upgrade and/or other reasons that may contain electronic data meeting the criteria listed in paragraph 1 above.

5. **Fixed Drives on Stand-Alone Personal Computers and Network Workstations:** With regard to electronic data meeting the criteria listed in paragraph 1 above, which existed on fixed drives attached to stand-alone microcomputers and/or network workstations at the time of this letter's delivery: Your client {clients} is {are} not to alter or erase such electronic data, and not to perform other procedures (such as data compression and disk de-fragmentation or optimization routines) that may impact such data, unless a true and correct copy has been made of such active files and of completely restored versions of such deleted electronic files and file fragments, copies have been made of all directory listings (including hidden files) for all directories and subdirectories containing such files, and arrangements have been made to preserve copies during the pendency of this litigation.

6. **Programs and Utilities:** Your client {clients} is {are} to preserve copies of all application programs and utilities, which may be used to process electronic data covered by this letter.

7. **Log of System Modifications:** Your client {clients} is {are} to maintain an activity log to document modifications made to any electronic data processing system that may affect the system's capability to process any electronic data meeting the criteria listed in paragraph 1 above, regardless of whether such modifications were made by employees, contractors, vendors and/or any other third parties.

8. **Personal Computers Used by Your Employees and/or Their Secretaries and Assistants:** The following steps should immediately be taken in regard to all personal computers used by your client's {clients'} employees and/or their secretaries and assistants.

   a. As to fixed drives attached to such computers: (i) a true and correct copy is to be made of all electronic data on such fixed drives relating to this matter, including all active files and completely restored versions of all deleted electronic files and file fragments; (ii) full directory listings (including hidden files) for all directories and subdirectories (including hidden directories) on such fixed drives should be written; and (iii) such copies and listings are to be preserved until this matter reaches its final resolution.

   b. All floppy diskettes, magnetic tapes and cartridges, and other media used in connection with such computers prior to the date of delivery of this letter containing any electronic data relating to this matter are to be collected and put into storage for the duration of this lawsuit.

9. **Evidence Created Subsequent to This Letter:** With regard to electronic data created subsequent to the date of delivery of this letter, relevant evidence is not be destroyed and your client {clients} is {are} to take whatever steps are appropriate to avoid destruction of evidence.

In order to assure that your and your client's {clients'} obligation to preserve documents and things will be met, please forward a copy of this letter to all persons and entities with custodial responsibility for the items referred to in this letter. We expect that you will monitor compliance.

Sincerely, etc.

Sample Electronic Discovery Interrogatories and Requests for Production

Below are suggested interrogatories and requests for production that are meant to be complementary (i.e., any devices or electronic files that are identified in answer to an interrogatory or interrogatories are usually immediately requested in the follow-up request[s] for production).

For more detailed questions that you might want to include in interrogatories rather than in a deposition, see the sample deposition questions.

Sample Interrogatories and Requests for Production

[Note: The precise format for the following suggested interrogatories and requests for production of documents and things should be in accordance with the applicable civil and local rules of the court where the matter is filed.]

[suggested language for inclusion in preamble:]

I. Definitions

For the purposes of the following interrogatories and requests for production of documents and things, the following definitions apply:

Application Software: A set of electronic instructions, also known as a program, which instructs a computer to perform a specific set of processes.

Archive: A copy of data on a computer drive, or on a portion of a drive, maintained for historical reference.

Backup: A copy of active data, intended for use in restoration of data.

Computer: Includes but is not limited to network servers, desktops, laptops, notebook computers, employees' home computers, mainframes, the PDAs of [party name] and its employees (personal digital assistants, such as PalmPilot, Blackberry and other such handheld computing devices), digital cell phones and pagers.

Data: Any and all information stored on media that may be accessed by a computer.

Digital Camera: A camera that stores still or moving pictures in a digital format (jpg, GIF, etc.).

Document: Includes but is not limited to any electronically stored data on magnetic or optical storage media as an "active" file or files (readily readable by one or more computer applications or forensics software); any "deleted" but recoverable electronic files on said media; any electronic file fragments (files that have been deleted and partially overwritten with new data); and slack (data fragments stored randomly from random access memory on a hard drive during the normal operation of a computer [RAM slack] or residual data left on the hard drive after new data has overwritten some but not all of previously stored data).

Hard Drive: The primary hardware that a computer uses to store information, typically magnetized media on rotating disks.

Help Features/Documentation: Instructions that assist a user on how to set up and use a product including but not limited to software, manuals and instruction files.

Imaged Copy: A "mirror image" bit-by-bit copy of a hard drive (i.e., a complete replication of the physical drive).

Input Device: Any object that allows a user to communicate with a computer by entering information or issuing commands (e.g., keyboard, mouse or joystick).

Magnetic or Optical Storage Media: Include but are not limited to hard drives (also known as "hard disks"), backup tapes, CD-ROMs, DVD-ROMs, JAZ and Zip drives, smart cards, memory sticks, digital jukeboxes, and floppy disks.

Network: A group of connected computers that allow people to share information and equipment (e.g., local area network [LAN], wide area network [WAN], metropolitan area network [MAN], storage area network [SAN], peer-to-peer network, client-server network).

Operating System: Software that directs the overall activity of a computer (e.g., MS-DOS, Windows, Linux).

Network Operating System: Software that directs the overall activity of networked computers.

Software: Any set of instructions stored on computer-readable media that tells a computer what to do. Includes operating systems and applications.

Storage Devices: Any device that a computer uses to store information.

Storage Media: Storage media are any removable devices that store data.

II. Spoliation: getting information on preservation of information.

S1. Written policies on preservation of records

Interrogatory No._____:

Do you have a written policy for the retention of documents, including but not limited to business records?

Request for Production No._____:

Please produce copies of any and all written policies for the retention of documents, for the time period of _____ to _____ inclusive.

S2. Destruction of documents

Interrogatory No._____:

Do you have a written policy for the destruction of documents, including but not limited to business records?

Request for Production No._____:

Please produce copies of any and all written policies for the destruction of documents, for the time period of _____ to _____ inclusive.

Interrogatory No._____:

Has destruction or overwriting of documents been suspended? If so, on what date did suspension begin?

S3. Persons in charge of maintaining document retention and destruction policies

Interrogatory No._____:

Identified by job title, job description and business address and telephone number, who are all persons in charge of implementing the policies identified in your answer to Interrogatories 1 and 2 above?

Interrogatory No._____ :

If not the same person(s) as identified in your answer to the immediately preceding interrogatory, identify by job title, job description, and business address and telephone number, the person at [party name] who is the most knowledgeable about the retention and destruction of documents at [party name]?

Interrogatory No._____:

With respect to preventing the spoliation of documents and things that may potentially become evidence in litigation, please identify with particularity and in detail:

  a. Whether the minutes of the meetings of the Board of Directors, from [date] to [date] contain any references to considerations or discussions of preventing such spoliation of potential evidence.

  b. If so, state the dates of the meetings for which minutes were taken.

  c. If so, state the name, title, job description, business address and telephone number of the person or persons with custody of those minutes.

Request for Production No._____:

Please produce all documents referenced in the immediately preceding interrogatory.

S4. Preservation of evidence

Interrogatory No._____:

Since [date of opposing party's awareness of client's claim or counterclaim, if not date of complaint, cross-claim or counterclaim], have any documents at [party name] been destroyed? If so, please state which electronic files have been deleted from the magnetic or optical storage media of [party name] or overwritten from that date to the present, and dates of destruction or overwriting.

S5. Storage of documents

Interrogatory No._____:

As to the storage of data generated by the users of your computers (such as word-processed files and email), please state whether:

A. The data are backed up on tape or other media?

1. If so:

    a. How many such media currently exist with backup data on them?
    b. What is the maximum storage size in megabytes for each such media?
    c. What is the brand name for each such media?
    d. When was the last time each such media was backed up with data?
    e. What was the computer or other hardware (e.g., individual workstation, server) for each such backup?
    f. With respect to the immediately foregoing question, state the physical location and current user of each computer or other hardware listed.

Request for Production No._____:

Please produce all backup and/or archive media, for the time period of _____ to _____ inclusive.

III. Data Universe — identifying it

Interrogatory No._____:

Does or did [party name] maintain, or contract with another party to maintain, an overall inventory of data resources such as a Year 2000 Plan, a 9/11 Recovery Plan or Disaster Recovery Plan? If so, please provide the name, address, phone number and other contact information for the individuals primarily responsible for maintenance of the inventory and/or plan.

Request No._____:

Produce any and all company organizational and policy information in its entirety, including but not limited to organizational charts, corporate policy and procedure manuals, policy memoranda, system schematic, network topology, system restart procedures, email retention policies, Year 2000 Plan, a 9/11 Recovery Plan, Disaster Recovery Plan, and other related items.

IV. Information Personnel

Interrogatory No._____:

Provide a list of all personnel responsible for maintaining computer hardware, data or information systems on computers for [party name]. Include name, position title, contact information, and official job description and list of duties.

Request No._____:

Produce all formal and informal contact lists and duty rosters for personnel in Information Technology (IT) and Information Services (IS), or equivalent divisions within [party name]. Specifically include rosters for groups such as Incident Response Teams, Data Recovery Units, Audit/Investigation Teams, etc.

Request No._____:

Produce all formal job descriptions, assignments and personnel lists for IT and IS personnel, including revisions, for the period _____ to _____.

V. Loose Media (including Backup and Archive)

Interrogatory No._____:

Does [party name] maintain a policy regarding use of loose or removable media in its workstations, computers or networks? If so, state the name of the person(s) responsible for creating and enforcing that policy.

Request No._____:

Provide a copy of the policy mentioned in the preceding interrogatory, as well as any revisions, records or logs related to formulation or enforcement of that policy for the period _____ to _____.

Request No._____:

Produce any and all devices used to place information on loose or removable storage media, including but not limited to hard drives, floppy drives, CD-ROM drives, tape drives, recordable DVD-ROM drives, and removable drives. Include all instructions for use and maintenance of those devices.

Request No._____:

Produce any and all loose or removable media used to store data, including but not limited to floppy disks, CD-ROM discs and tape drive cartridges, that have been used by personnel or contractors of [party name] to perform work for [party name].

Request No._____:

Produce any and all backup and/or archived data [describe scope of data].

Request No._____:

All slack, wherever located, even if media contains nonproduced data.

VI. Computer Hardware

(most appropriate for forensics work or when a motion to compel must be used to gather opponent's data)

Interrogatory No._____:

List all computer equipment provided by [party name] or used by employees of [party name] to perform work for [party name], including but not limited to hardware and/or peripherals attached to a computer such as computer cases [desktop, tower, portable/batteries, all-in-one], monitors, modems [internal, external], printers, keyboards, printers, scanners, mice [cord and cordless], pointing devices [joystick, touchpad, trackball] and speakers. Include description of equipment, serial number, all users for the period _____ to _____ and dates used, and all locations where the equipment was located for the period _____ to _____.

Interrogatory No._____:

Will [party name] permit, without an order therefore, inspection of the equipment mentioned in the preceding interrogatory?

Request No. [follow-up, if response to preceding interrogatory is negative] _____:

Please produce the following computers, including their magnetic or optical storage media, for inspection and copying, on or before [date], at the offices of [law firm] at [address]:

[list of computers you want image-copied, previously identified in discovery; alternatively, if you know the computer population is relatively small]:

Please produce your computers, including their magnetic or optical storage media, for inspection and copying, on or before [date], at the offices of [law firm] at [address]:

Interrogatory No._____:

List all hardware components (e.g., motherboard, modem, NIC, etc.) installed internally or externally to the PC(s) used by _____ during the period _____ to _____.

Request No._____:

Provide any and all documentation of software and hardware modifications to the PC(s) used by _____ during the period _____ to _____, including but not limited to modification dates, software/hardware titles and version numbers, names of persons performing modifications, location of any backup of the data on the computer performed prior to modification, and disposition of replaced software and hardware.

Request No._____:

Produce any and all documentation instructing in setup and use of the PC(s) used by _____ during the period _____ to _____, and hardware and software installed on that/those PC(s). Include any and all documentation reflecting communication with a computer professional or help desk for help in setting up and using the PC(s).

Interrogatory No._____:

List discarded or replaced hardware and software for the PC(s) (including entire PCs) used by _____ during the period _____ to _____. If the hardware or software is no longer in your control, then include the name and contact information of last known custodian.

VII. Computer Software

Request No._____:

Produce any and all software installed or used on the PC(s) used by _____ during the period _____ to _____. Include all titles and version numbers. Include authors and contact information for authors of custom or customized software. Include operating system(s) software.

VIII. Operating Systems

Interrogatory No._____:

List all operating systems (including but not limited to UNIX, Windows, DOS, Linux and PDA operating systems) installed on all computers used by [party name], the specific equipment the OS was installed on and the period during which it was installed on the specific equipment.

Request No._____:

Provide copies of all operating system software listed in the preceding interrogatory, and all supporting documentation provided with the software, and any manuals and tutorials acquired by [party name] to support use of the software.

IX. Telephony

Interrogatory No._____:

Do you have any graphic representation of the components of your telephone and voice messaging system, and the relationship of those components to each other, including but not limited to flow charts, videos or photos, and diagrams?

Interrogatory No._____:

If so, where are the documents located? Include logical paths for electronic documents.

Request No._____:

Produce copies of any and all graphic representations of your telephone and voice messaging network, and the relationship of those components to each other, including any revisions, for the period of _____ to _____ inclusive. If the documents are electronic, please produce them in their native form, as they existed at the time they were drafted, based on archive or back-up data.

Interrogatory No._____:

List all telephone equipment provided by [party name] or used by employees of [party name] to perform work for [party name], including but not limited to desktop telephones, cell phones, pagers, PDA and laptop modems, calling cards, telephony software and contact management software. Include description of equipment and software, serial number, all users for the period of _____ to _____ inclusive and dates used, and all locations where the equipment was located for the period of _____ to _____ inclusive.

Interrogatory No._____:

Will [party name] permit, without an order therefore, inspection of the equipment mentioned in the preceding interrogatory?

Request No._____:

Produce any and all voice messaging records including but not limited to caller message recordings, digital voice recordings, interactive voice response unit (IVR/VRU) recordings, unified messaging files, and computer-based voice mail files to or from [specified parties] for the period _____ to _____.

Request No._____:

Produce all phone use records for [party name] including but not limited to logs of incoming and outgoing calls, invoices and contact management records, manually or automatically created or generated for the period from _____ to _____ inclusive.

X. Other Sources of Electronic Evidence

Interrogatory No._____:

List all log files (files with suffixes) found on computers in [party name]'s network, and the equipment and logical path where the log files may be found.

Request No._____:

Provide copies of the following log files: [this is a follow-up request to the preceding interrogatory, issued after the list of log files has been reviewed]

Request No._____:

Produce any and all manual and automatic records of equipment use, including but not limited to fax, access, audit, security, email, printing, error and transmission records.

Interrogatory No._____:

Do any employees of [party name] subscribe to or participate in Internet newsgroups or chat groups in the course of their employment? If so, list all users and the services that they subscribe to or participate in.

Request No._____:

Produce any and all information related to newsgroups or chat groups, including but not limited to names and passwords for each and every service, newsgroup messages, text files and programs used to access messages.

Interrogatory No._____:

Do any employees of [party name] use portable devices in the course of their employment that are not connected to [party name]'s network, and that are not backed up or archived? If so, list all users and the devices they use.

Request No._____:

Produce any and all portable devices not backed up or archived, including but not limited to handheld devices, set-top boxes, notebook devices, CE devices, digital recorders, digital cameras and external storage devices.

Interrogatory No._____:

Does [party name] provide Internet access for any of its employees or has [party name] done so at any time during the period from _____ to _____ inclusive? If so, list the employees who had Internet access, the Internet service provider (ISP) used, and describe the method(s) used to connect to the Internet.

Request No._____:

Produce any and all documentation describing installation and use of hardware and software used by [party name] to provide Internet access for its employees during the period from _____ to _____ inclusive.

Request No._____:

Produce copies of all manuals, policies and other guidelines for employee access and use of Internet resources.

Interrogatory No._____:

Describe any restrictions on, controls over or monitoring of employee use of Internet resources.

Request No._____:

Provide any records generated as a result of restrictions on, controls over and monitoring of employee use of Internet resources.

Interrogatory No._____:

Provide a list of any and all Internet-related data on the PCs used by [specific employees or classes of employees], including but not limited to saved Web pages, lists of Web sites, URL addresses, Web browser software and settings, bookmarks, favorites, history lists, caches, cookies.

XI. Data Security Measures

Interrogatory No._____:

List any and all user identification numbers and passwords necessary to access computers or programs addressed in interrogatories and requests. Your response to this interrogatory must be updated with responses to future sets of interrogatories and requests and updated responses to any set of interrogatories and requests.

Interrogatory No._____: ·

Please provide copies of your computer security policies and procedures and the name and contact information for the person responsible for security.

Interrogatory No._____:

Please provide information about the security settings for the [program]. For example, please provide the security settings for the Exchange Server, noting who has administrative rights.

XII. Network Questions

Request No._____:

Produce any and all documents and things related to networks or groups of connected computers that allow people to share information and equipment, including but not limited to local area networks (LANs), wide area networks (WANs), metropolitan area networks (MANs), storage area networks (SANs), peer-to-peer networks, client-server networks, integrated services digital networks and VPNs.

Request No._____:

Produce any and all components related to networks, including but not limited to information exchange components (e.g., Ethernet, token-ring, ATM), network work file servers, traffic, hubs, network interface cards, cables, firewalls, user names, passwords and intranet.

N1. System overview

Interrogatory No._____:

Do you have any graphic representation of the components of your computer network, and the relationship of those components to each other, including but not limited to flow charts, videos or photos, and drawings? Include network topology documents and network schemas in your response.

Interrogatory No._____:

If so, where are the documents located? Include logical paths and physical locations for electronic representations.

Request No._____:

Produce copies of any and all graphic representations of your computer network, and the relationship of those components to each other, including any revisions, for the period of _____ to _____ inclusive. If the documents are electronic, produce them in their native form, as they existed at the time they were drafted, based on version or backup data.

XIII. Electronic Mail (email)

Request No._____:

Produce any and all information related to email, including but not limited to current, backed-up and archived programs, accounts, unified messaging, server-based email, web-based email, dial-up email, user names and addresses, domain names and addresses, email messages, attachments, manual and automated mailing lists and mailing list addresses.

Appendix E: Sample 30(b)(6) Deposition Questions

Questions to Ask at the 30(b)(6) Deposition of the Designated IT Person

The following questions may be useful to ask of the deponent in order to track down the sources of electronic data relevant to your case. The broad non-technical questions are meant to be foundational to the technical ones.

Depending on your jurisdiction's limitation on interrogatories, most of the following questions can be used first in interrogatories, with follow-ups wherever necessary in depositions and requests for production.

These questions are crafted to assist you in getting focused, specific answers. Whether you ask these questions or others, of course, is up to you. You are far more familiar with the specific issues of your case, and our charge is not to provide you with legal but rather technical advice. You may wish to have an electronic discovery expert process you and/or your witness, depending on what side of the table you find yourself.

Otherwise, after you have had the deposition transcribed, an e-discovery expert can help you assess the responses you were given for completeness and accuracy.

Personnel:

1. To whom at your company do you report?
2. Who works directly under you?

3. Does your company have an organizational chart? Who has custody of such a chart?

4. How many people at your company have a direct responsibility for computers and/or networks?

5. What are their job titles and duties?

6. What outsourced services, if any, do you use in the care and maintenance of your company's computer hardware, software or network(s)?

7. Who is the person at your company who is ultimately responsible for responding to discovery requests made of your attorney(s) in this lawsuit? If you are not that person, what role, if any, did you play in responding to discovery requests made of your attorney(s) in this lawsuit?

8. What have you done to prepare for your deposition here today?

9. What documents did you review prior to your deposition here today?

Systems information:

1. Do you use a computer or computers at work? If so, how many?

   a. Is the computer on your desk?
   b. Do you know the brand name?
   c. Does it run on Windows?
      — If so, Windows 3.1, 95, 98, 2000 or NT?
      — If not, is it a Unix-based system? Linux? Macintosh? Apple?
   d. Are you the only person with access to this computer?
      — If not, who else uses it?
      — If not, who else has access to it?
   e. Has this computer ever been used in the past by anyone else?
      — If so, who?
   f. Who keeps the records of purchases of equipment, such as your computer?
   g. When and where was your computer bought?
   h. Does it have a hard drive? More than one? Do you know what its/their storage capacity is in gigabytes?
   i. Do you need to use a password to access the computer? If so, what is the password? How often have you changed that password?
   j. Does the computer have a floppy disk drive? A CD-ROM drive?
   k. Is your computer capable of saving files on an external drive?
   l. Is your computer equipped with software to transfer files from one computer to another?

m. Is your computer equipped with remote access software?

n. Is it connected in such a way as to be able to access the Internet and send and receive e-email?

o. Do you ever backup anything from your computer? If so, how, how often, the times of the last two backups, and on what kind of media (floppy disk, other disk drive, onto the server, memory stick, CD-ROM, streaming backup tape media, [other -- if so, what?])

p. Do you ever make "personal" copies of files or other data from your computer (work station)? If so, when? Why? How often? Where are those copies? How many are at work? How many at home or elsewhere?

q. Do you use a laptop, notebook computer or personal data assistant such as a PalmPilot, Pocket PC, Blackberry or other portable computer? How are data moved back and forth between these devices and your computer (work station)?

r. Do you use a computer at home? [if so, repeat relevant questions above as to type, kind, features, backups, who else has access to it, etc.]

s. Have you received or sent email from your home computer?

t. Have you worked on your home computer to do work for your company?

u. Has your employer paid for all or a part of your home computer?

Network Information:

1. Is the computer you use at work connected to a network? What kind of network is it (LAN, WAN, intranet)? If so, do you know what your access rights are? (translation: level of security to access files, the top access right being "administrator" in most systems)

   a. What is your password to get onto the network?

   b. Who else knows your password?

   c. Do you know what a server is? [if not, have him/her assume it is the main computer to which all the work station (client) desktop computers are connected] Is your computer connected to a server?

   d. Is there more than one server in the network?

   e. Under what operating system does the server work (e.g. Windows NT, Novell, Unix, Linux)? What version?

   f. Do you have a network administrator whose job it is to make sure the network keeps running properly or who can fix it when it does not? If not, whose job is that?

g. Is there an Information Services or Information Technology department in your company? Who are those people and who is the person in charge?

h. Is there somebody in charge of doing backups of data from the server? If so, who?

i. Do you know how often the network server is backed up? If not, are you aware that there is a backup system in place? If not, what is your understanding as to how your company's computer data will be preserved in the event of a disaster, such as a fire, flood, theft or vandalism?

j. Do you know what kind of backup hardware and software are used? If so, what specific hardware and software, and version of that software? If not: who would most likely know the answers to this question?

Email and Software Usage:

1. Do you send and receive email from your computer? If so, what email program(s) do you use? (If he/she does not know, suggest Microsoft Exchange/Outlook, Lotus CC:Mail, Groupwise or Eudora as possibilities).

2. Do you know how received mail is routed in your company? Does your company have document management software to log incoming and/or outgoing mail? If not, is there a policy on how incoming mail is logged and routed? How often do you delete your incoming email from your work station? Outgoing email? When is the last time you did that? And the time before that?

3. How often do you delete your incoming email from the server? Outgoing email? When is the last time you did that? And the time before that?

4. Do you know if your email is backed up from time to time, either from your desktop computer or from the network server?

5. Have you ever printed out an email message? If so, how often, when, and for what purpose?

6. Have you ever archived your email? If so, how?

7. What word processing software do you use? Is this the same software used by everyone else in the company, to your knowledge? Was there at any time a different word processing program used by the company? If so, when was/were the conversion(s) made? Have you ever archived your word processing documents? If so, where?

8. Repeat question 7 as to spreadsheet program (such as Excel); database management program (such as Microsoft Access); presentation software (such as PowerPoint); Personal Information Management software (such as Outlook); contact management software (such as Act!).
9. What other software do you use in your work?
10. Do you do your own word processing? If not, who does?
11. Do you maintain your own calendar? If not, who does?
12. If you have a PalmPilot, Pocket PC or other handheld data device, do you keep your calendar on it? How far does it go back? What other data do you keep on such a device?

Preservation of Evidence:

1. Once this lawsuit was brought, did anyone tell you to preserve all your electronic data and not erase any of it? Since [commencement of lawsuit], have you deleted any files from your computer?
2. Have you been asked by anyone since [commencement of lawsuit] to delete any files on any computer to which you have access, whether at work or at home or elsewhere?
3. Do you know what it is to "defragment" your computer? If so, have you ever run such a program to defragment it?
4. Do you know what it means to "wipe" a hard drive? If so, have you ever run software that will "wipe" a drive? Where? When? Why?
5. Does your company have a written email policy concerning such matters as prohibited content, statement of who owns the email, expectations of privacy, or any other policy relating to email? If so, how long has that policy been in place? How many times has it been amended? Who is the author of the current policy? Do you have a copy of the policy?
6. Does your company have a written policy concerning the retention and destruction of paper records? If so, how long has that policy been in place? How many times has it been amended? Who is the author of the current policy? Do you have a copy of the policy?
7. Does your company have a written policy concerning the retention and destruction of electronic records (such as files generated by computers, voice mail, email)? If so, how long has that policy been in place? How many times has it been amended? Who is the author of the current policy? Do you have a copy of the policy?
8. Does your company have a disaster recovery plan? A Y2K plan? Did your company have a plan around 9/11 events?

Third-party sources of information:

1. Are there places outside the physical location of your company where you regularly send email or other electronic files, such as a parent company, subsidiary, outside consultants, government entities, investors, other parties to this lawsuit [hereinafter = "outside entity"]? If so, to whom, when and why?

2. Who are the persons at [outside entity] who regularly send you email? What are their functions and what purposes does each person's email serve (i.e. in terms of their job function)?

3. Have you seen what kind of computers the [outside entity] uses?

4. Can you estimate how many computers there are there?

5. Are they networked?

6. Does the [outside entity] direct you or otherwise expect you to use compatible software?

7. [If foreign entity] Do you know how much of what they generate internally is in English and how much is in [foreign language]?

8. Do you know how received mail is routed in the [outside entity]? Does [outside entity] have document management software to log incoming and/or outgoing mail? Do you have such software? If not, is there a policy on how incoming mail is logged and routed? Does this policy come from [outside entity]?

9. Have you ever been told by anyone in [outside entity] that they did not receive mail you had sent them? To your knowledge, has lost mail been a problem expressed to you by [outside entity]?

10. Who else besides you receives email from the [outside entity]?

11. Besides email, have you ever exchanged documents in electronic form between your company and the [outside entity]? If so, have you ever done so by attaching documents to email? Any other way?

12. Are faxes routinely sent back and forth between you and [outside entity]?

13. Is there a fax log kept of these incoming and outgoing faxes?

14. Do you have such a log kept on a computer? If so, how is that log kept and by what software?

15. In sending or receiving a fax between you and [outside entity], has there ever been a fax sent electronically, i.e. from a computer without use of paper? Is that the typical way faxes are sent? (if appropriate: If not, what if anything explains why sometimes a fax would be sent electronically and why at other times by paper?)

16. Have you received any emails from [outside entity] concerning this lawsuit?

17. Have you been told by anyone at [outside entity] to do anything with information in your possession or to which you have access, such as to preserve it, destroy it, or anything else?

18. Have you received from or sent emails to anyone in [outside entity] in the last ____ years?

19. Have you deleted from your office or home computer(s) any of that email? If so, what and when?

20. Do you have a secretary or assistant who processes documents for you? Does he or she have a computer? [If so, you may want to repeat questions above about type of computer, whether networked, types of software used, configuration and features, whether he/she keeps duplicate or backup files from his/her computer]

21. Does your company have voice mail? Are voice mails stored and retained? Do you receive voice mail from time to time from [outside entity]?

22. What is the most often-used medium of document exchange between [outside entity]and you: email, fax, regular mail, or something else?

23. How frequent are your communications with [outside entity] (i.e. daily, once a week, monthly)? Has there ever been a significant period of time (i.e. more than ____ weeks) when there was no communication between you and [outside entity]? If so, was that, if you know, due to technical problems of any kind, such as computer system failures?

24. Do you have any communications with [outside entity] through use of collaborative software, such as "white boarding" over the Internet with something like Microsoft's NetMeeting, or through use of a Web site where people can meet via the Internet and share ideas and thoughts?

25. Is there a site on the Internet where you and [outside entity] post and share information?

26. Is there a site not on the Internet (such as an intranet or extranet) where you and the [outside entity] post and share information?

27. Does [outside entity] have a Web site? If so, what is its Internet address?

28. In conjunction with this lawsuit, has anyone at [outside entity] asked you to look for records or otherwise supply information, either in paper or electronic form? If so, what documents, when, and for what stated purpose?

Storage:

1. Where are backup tapes stored in your company (physical location)?
2. What security measures are in place to protect unauthorized access to those tapes?
3. Are backups kept on anything other than tapes?
4. What person or persons have custody of those tapes?
5. Who makes the backups? How long has that person been doing that? Who did the backups before that person?
6. What is the brand name and type of backup tape?
7. Are the backup tapes labeled? If so, what information is kept on the labels?
8. Have any backup tapes ever been destroyed, erased or altered, to your knowledge? If so, when, where and why?

Records Management:

1. Do you have a records management (RM) or Enterprise Content Management (ECM) system?
2. Have you used your records management or ECM system?
3. Who administers your records management or ECM system?
4. Do you choose what documents to put into the records management system or ECM system?
5. Do you choose the categorization for the RM or ECM system?
6. Can you check documents in and out of the RM or ECM system?
7. Do you keep documents in places other than the RM or ECM system? Where?

Other Lawsuits:

1. Has your company ever produced electronic data to another party in a lawsuit? If so, in what matter? What data was produced? In what format was the electronic data produced (e.g. on CD-ROMs, floppies, printouts?)
2. To what party or parties was that data produced? Was any of the electronic data used at trial? In support of any motions?
3. What was/were the caption of that case/those cases, and filed with what court(s)?

Retired Hardware:

1. What is the usual life span of a computer at your company?
2. Is there a practice of computers used at one echelon of the company (for example, top management) migrating to other employees in the company as newer equipment is purchased?
3. What happens to computers and/or their hard drives when they are retired from service?
4. How many computers from _____ to _____ were retired from service, given away or sold? Who would have records that might answer that question? What would you call such records for the purpose of being able to identify them?

Encryption and Legacy Data:

1. Is encryption (encoding of data that prevents accessing it without a proper decoding or decryption software or hardware key) used in any of the following:
   a. emails
   b. data stored on servers
   c. data stored on backups
   d. data generated by any software application
   e. other

If so, state the type of encryption used, the name(s) of any software used, the level of encryption, and how, for each instance, the process for decryption of the data works.

2. Do you maintain electronic data on backup tapes, archive tapes, hard drives, or otherwise, for which you no longer actively use the software to read the data on those storage media? [This question is meant to elicit information about "legacy data," electronic data on such old software programs as WordStar, VisiCalc or WANG] If so, do you still have the old software and user manuals? Who in your company would know how to recover that data?

Appendix F: Data Collection Forms

Receipt of Media Form

Prepared at the request of counsel – privileged and confidential

Received from:

Name _____ Title _____

Address _____

City _____ State _____ Zip _____

Phone (w) _____ Ext _____

Phone (h) _____ Ext _____

Cell _____ Pager _____ Pin _____

Email _____

Media Type	Serial Number	Notes

Released to:

Name _____ Title _____

Signature _____ Date _____

Phone (w) _____ Ext _____

Phone (h) _____ Ext _____

Email _____

© *Copyright 2000-2005, Fios, Inc.*

Desktop Collection Information Form

Prepared at the request of counsel – privileged and confidential

The information below will assist in describing the chain of custody for the data which is collected.

Computer user:

Name_____

Email_____

Address _____

City_____State_____Zip_____

Phone (w)_____Ext _____

Phone (h) _____Ext _____

Cell _____Pager_____Pin _____

Title _____ISID_____

Brought to you? Y/N   If yes, by whom?

Name_____

Phone (w)_____Ext _____

Phone (h) _____Ext _____

If not brought to you:

Building_____Floor _____Office/Cube/Mailstop_____

Was this the only computer in this person's area? Y/N _____

Location of computer (ex. On desk, under desk, in leather bag)

_____

Machine/drive identifiers:

Type (Laptop, desktop, notebook, server) _____

Manufacturer_____

Model_____Serial Number _____

Asset/inventory tag _____

Number of peripherals attached to the computer with the computer
of interest (write 0 if none) Also, removable media in area:
Hard drives _____CD ROM Read Only___
CD Rom Read/Write_____Fax/modem_____
3.5 floppy_____Printer ports _____
Zip/Jaz drive _____USB ports _____
Docking station _____Network connection_____
Floppies _____Tapes _____
CD Roms _____Zip, Jaz _____
Other not listed _____

Notes: _____

Bios date/time _____**Actual date/time** _____

Name of Ghost image_____

Copied to network drive _____

Type of data	Name	Date collected	Collected by
Home directory			
User computer			
Email			
Share 1			
Share 2			

(Continue on back of sheet)

Gatherer's information and signature:

Signature _____

Name_____

Gathered at the request of_____

Case identifier _____

© Copyright 2000-2005, Fios, Inc.

Server Information Form

Prepared at the request of counsel-privileged and confidential

Location: _____Server _____

On site contact:

Name _____Title _____

Address _____

City_____State _____Zip _____

Phone (w)_____Ext _____

Phone (h) _____Ext _____

Cell _____Pager _____Pin _____

Email (w)_____

Email (h) _____

Physical Location:
Secure location? Y/N If yes, type of access (e.g. Keycard, code)

_____

Phone (in room)_____Ext _____

Building _____Floor _____Room _____

Location of computer (e.g. Rack #, Shelf)

_____

Hardware:
Machine name_____

Manufacturer _____

Domain name _____

Model_____Serial # _____

Asset tag #_____

Tape drive manufacturer _____

Model #_____Serial # _____

Tape media size _____

Time:
Bios date/time_____

Actual date/time _____

Time zone_____

Daylight savings selected? _____

Software:
Operating system version and service pack

_____

Exchange version and service pack

_____

Site name_____

Organization name _____

Exmerge version _____

Backup software/version_____

Open file agent? _____

Gather's information and signature:

Name _____Title _____

Signature _____

Company_____

Phone (w)_____Ext _____

Phone (h) _____Ext _____

Email (w)_____

Email (h) _____

© *Copyright 2000-2005, Fios, Inc.*

Key Personnel List

Prepared at the request of counsel-privileged and confidential

Location : _____

Role	Name/Department	Phone/Email
Top Manager		
Top IT Manager		
Email		
Network		
Desktop		
Security		
Help Desk		
Telecom		
Human Resources		

© *Copyright 2000-2005, Fios, Inc.*

ABOUT THE AUTHORS

Mary Mack, Esq, *Technology Counsel*

Whether in response to an inquiry, a 2nd request or class action litigation, Mary brings legal and technical professionals together in a focused manner to determine a successful, cost effective course of compliance with electronic data requests. The Director of Solution Design for Discovery Management Services for Fios, she has twenty years experience delivering enterprise wide software projects with IT departments in Fortune 100 companies. Mary has assisted counsel, IT and litigation support professionals identify, reduce, gather, analyze and produce over 1500 terabytes of data. Clients include the largest law firms, pharmaceutical, financial and insurance companies in the world.

A member of the Illinois Bar, ACCA and the ABA's Section on Litigation, Mary received her J.D. from Northwestern University School of Law (1982) and a B.A. from LeMoyne College in Syracuse, NY. She holds certifications in Computer Forensics and Computer Telephony.

Steve Pattison, *VP of Alliances and Business Development, Interwoven, Inc.*

Steve Pattison is responsible for all third party relationships at Interwoven, including Systems Integrator, Technology, and OEM/VAR relationships. He has more than 12 years experience in the ECM industry working with software and Global Consulting organizations.

Pattison joined Interwoven via the merge with iManage, Inc. in November, 2003. Steve served as vice president of alliances and business development for iManage, Inc., establishing key partnerships that expanded the company's position as the leader in Collaborative Document Management. Previously, Pattison served as the vice president of technology partnerships for Documentum, Inc., where he was one of the early innovators of the Enterprise Content Management space. Steve served as vice president of business development and services for Plumtree Software, growing the organization from start-up to a publicly traded company and leader in the Portal software arena. Prior to entering the software industry, Steve worked for PriceWaterhouseCoopers for seven years, building their SAP and related practices internationally.

Steve holds a BS in MIS and Marketing from the University of Minnesota and an MBA from the Wharton School of Management.

Lincoln Township Public Library
2099 W. John Beers Rd.
Stevensville, MI 49127
(269) 429-9575

Printed in the United States
42161LVS00002B/238-291